How to Be Better

CRAFTED BY SKRIUWER

Copyright © 2024 by Skriuwer.

All rights reserved. No part of this book may be used or reproduced in any form whatsoever without written permission except in the case of brief quotations in critical articles or reviews.

For more information, contact : **kontakt@skriuwer.com** (www.skriuwer.com)

TABLE OF CONTENTS

CHAPTER 1: INTRODUCTION: WHAT DOES IT MEAN TO BE BETTER?

- *Being better is a journey, not a one-time event*
- *Small, steady steps lead to lasting improvement*
- *Recognizing strengths and weaknesses is the first step*

CHAPTER 2: UNDERSTANDING YOUR STARTING POINT

- *Self-reflection helps identify current habits and goals*
- *Honest assessment reveals areas for growth*
- *Journaling or talking to someone can clarify challenges*

CHAPTER 3: SETTING CLEAR AND MEANINGFUL GOALS

- *Use specific, measurable targets to guide progress*
- *Short-term and long-term goals keep motivation balanced*
- *Flexibility allows goals to evolve with changing needs*

CHAPTER 4: BUILDING SELF-DISCIPLINE

- *Discipline carries you when motivation is low*
- *Small habits repeated daily form strong routines*
- *Rewards and accountability can reinforce consistency*

CHAPTER 5: OVERCOMING FEARS AND DOUBTS

- *Facing fear gradually reduces its power*
- *Positive self-talk and support systems help build courage*
- *Reframing failure as learning fosters resilience*

CHAPTER 6: DEVELOPING HEALTHY HABITS

- *Regular exercise, balanced diet, and proper sleep boost well-being*
- *Mindful routines lower stress and increase energy*
- *Simple daily changes can lead to major benefits over time*

CHAPTER 7: GROWING THROUGH CHALLENGES AND FAILURE

- *Mistakes are opportunities to learn, not reasons to quit*
- *Persistence and adaptability develop real strength*
- *Reevaluating setbacks can uncover better strategies*

CHAPTER 8: LEARNING FROM OTHERS

- *Mentors and role models provide shortcuts to growth*
- *Observing different perspectives expands understanding*
- *Asking questions builds knowledge and stronger connections*

CHAPTER 9: NURTURING POSITIVE RELATIONSHIPS

- *Communication, empathy, and respect sustain healthy bonds*
- *Listening actively fosters deeper trust*
- *Quality time together strengthens emotional support*

CHAPTER 10: MANAGING TIME AND ENERGY

- *Effective scheduling and prioritizing tasks reduce overwhelm*
- *Short breaks and mindful pauses prevent burnout*
- *Distraction-free focus blocks boost daily productivity*

CHAPTER 11: STRENGTHENING SELF-CONFIDENCE

- *Challenging negative thoughts opens room for belief in yourself*
- *Stepping outside comfort zones builds lasting confidence*
- *Celebrating small wins sustains momentum*

CHAPTER 12: FINDING MOTIVATION EVERY DAY

- *Clear, meaningful goals spark internal drive*
- *Combining short rewards with long-term vision helps maintain focus*
- *Positive routines and recognizing progress create continuous motivation*

CHAPTER 13: BEING RESPONSIBLE FOR YOUR LIFE

- *Accepting accountability turns mistakes into lessons*
- *Choices shape outcomes; blaming others stalls progress*
- *Self-reliance balances asking for help when truly needed*

CHAPTER 14: EMBRACING GRATITUDE AND KINDNESS

- *Thankfulness changes perspective and boosts mental health*
- *Small acts of kindness ripple positively through communities*
- *Giving back and appreciating blessings enhance daily joy*

CHAPTER 15: COMMUNICATING CLEARLY AND RESPECTFULLY

- *Tone, word choice, and body language affect how messages are received*
- *Active listening creates deeper understanding*
- *Resolving conflict calmly preserves relationships*

CHAPTER 16: FACING STRESS AND ANXIETY

- *Identifying triggers and early warning signs aids quick response*
- *Techniques like deep breathing, grounding, or mindful breaks relieve tension*
- *Long-term habits (exercise, rest, reflection) build overall resilience*

CHAPTER 17: BALANCING WORK AND PERSONAL LIFE

- *Setting boundaries prevents burnout and preserves relationships*
- *Time management and realistic goals protect energy levels*
- *Regular check-ins ensure work does not overshadow personal well-being*

CHAPTER 18: ADAPTING TO CHANGE

- *Viewing each shift as a learning opportunity reduces fear*
- *Flexibility and open-mindedness help manage uncertainty*
- *Staying curious and maintaining routines create stability*

CHAPTER 19: CONTINUING PERSONAL GROWTH OVER A LIFETIME

- *Seeing growth as a journey keeps you learning at every age*
- *Reflecting honestly and adjusting goals prevents stagnation*
- *Overcoming plateaus involves new challenges, mentors, and varied methods*

CHAPTER 20: CONCLUSION: A NEW PATH FORWARD

- *Personal growth combines all lessons: discipline, kindness, resilience*
- *Small daily actions shape a meaningful, balanced life*
- *Growth is ongoing, transforming every stage of your life positively*

Chapter 1: Introduction: What Does It Mean to Be Better?

Section 1: The Basic Idea of Being Better

When we talk about "being better," we mean improving ourselves step by step. This can include different parts of our lives: our thoughts, our feelings, our actions, and our relationships with other people. It can also include how we take care of our health, how we deal with stress, how we make plans for the future, and so on. You might think that being better means becoming more successful, richer, or more famous. But true personal growth is not just about money or fame. It is about learning, growing, and making changes in ways that make you happier, healthier, and more fulfilled.

Some people think that if they make one big change in their lives, they will suddenly become a "better" person. But being better usually comes from many small steps and changes that build up over time. For example, if you want to be more patient, you might start by counting to five before you speak when you feel angry. If you want to be more caring, you might begin by doing a small favor for a friend or family member each day. These little actions add up. Eventually, you notice that you have become a more understanding, caring person.

Being better is also about understanding who you are right now. If you want to make progress, you first need to see your strengths and your weaknesses. You might be good at being creative but have a hard time staying organized. Or you might be kind to strangers but often fight with family members. Recognizing these things can help you set real goals for improvement.

It is also important to see that being better is a journey, not a single event. We don't suddenly wake up one day with no more problems or flaws. Instead, we learn to face our challenges and improve little by little. Even if we have a bad day, we can get up the next day and try again.

Children, teenagers, adults, and seniors can all improve themselves. It does not matter how old you are or what life situation you are in. There is always something you can do to grow. This might mean learning a new skill, changing the way you speak to others, or trying to be more open-minded about other people's opinions. Everyone's path is different, and that's okay.

In this book, we will talk about many areas of personal growth. We will look at topics like setting goals, becoming self-disciplined, handling fear, building healthy habits, and managing your time better. We will also talk about things like gratitude, responsibility, motivation, and learning from failure. The goal of this book is to help you see that you can always learn something new and that every step can make you a better person. You don't have to do everything at once, and you don't have to be perfect. You just have to keep going, one step at a time.

Section 2: Why We Should Want to Be Better

Many people ask, "Why should I bother trying to be better? If I'm okay right now, isn't that good enough?" This is a fair question. After all, personal growth takes time, energy, and often courage to face the parts of ourselves we don't like. But there are many reasons why it's worth it.

First, when we grow as individuals, we usually feel happier and more at peace. Growing isn't just about meeting some social expectation. It's about feeling that your life has purpose and direction. Imagine how good it feels to learn something new or to see yourself handle a difficult situation better than you would have in the past. These moments give us confidence and hope.

Second, personal growth helps us become better friends, parents, children, neighbors, and citizens. When we work on our weaknesses, we become easier to be around. We might argue less, listen more, and show more understanding. This improves our relationships and often leads to deeper connections with the people we care about.

Third, being better allows us to set meaningful goals for our future. If we drift through life without improving ourselves, we might feel stuck, bored, or frustrated. But if we keep moving forward and learning new things, we open doors to new opportunities. For example, if you develop good communication skills, you might find it easier to make friends or succeed in a job interview. If you learn to manage your time wisely, you can do better in school or at work.

Fourth, growth can help us handle hardships. Life can throw all kinds of problems our way—loss of a job, disagreements with friends, family issues, or even global events that affect our communities. If we keep pushing ourselves to develop qualities like patience, perseverance, and gratitude, we become more resilient. We can bounce back quicker from setbacks and not feel defeated so easily.

Fifth, working on ourselves can actually inspire others. Imagine you have a friend who wants to start exercising regularly, but they can't get motivated. If they see you—someone they know—actually making time for exercise and gradually getting stronger or healthier, that might motivate them to start as well. In this way, your personal growth can have a positive ripple effect on the people around you. You never know who is watching and learning from your example.

Finally, if we improve ourselves, we often come to understand our own values and beliefs more clearly. We learn what is truly important to us and what is just noise in the background. This helps us make better decisions and live in a way that feels right to us.

All these reasons show that striving to be better is not selfish or pointless. It's an investment in yourself and in the kind of world you want to live in. You don't have to tackle everything at once. Even small steps, taken consistently, can bring a lot of positive change over time. In the end, the reason to be better is that it makes your life richer, more fulfilling, and more meaningful.

Section 3: Common Myths About Self-Improvement

When you think about "self-improvement," you might picture reading many books, doing endless journaling, or taking seminars that promise quick fixes. You might also imagine a person who wakes up at 5 AM, meditates for an hour, runs 10 miles, and drinks only green smoothies. But while those habits can be good for some people, they are not the only way to grow. There are also some myths about self-improvement that can mislead us:

1. **Myth: You Have to Do It Alone.**
   Some people think self-improvement is a lonely path. They believe they need to lock themselves away and figure everything out on their own. In reality, you can learn and grow a lot from others. You can get help, join support groups, have mentors, or simply talk to friends who share your goals. Community can be a great source of motivation and knowledge.
2. **Myth: You Need a Perfect Plan.**
   Another myth is that you need the perfect plan or routine to be successful. The truth is no plan is perfect because life is unpredictable. You might set up a strict schedule, but then get sick or have a family emergency. The key is to remain flexible and adapt. A plan is just a guide to help you move forward, not a set of rules that must never change.
3. **Myth: It's All About Positive Thinking.**
   It is good to be optimistic. However, just thinking positively does not magically solve problems. Real growth means taking action. If you find yourself saying, "Everything will work out," but you do nothing to improve your situation, you might end up disappointed. Positive thinking can help keep you in the right mindset, but you still have to do the work.
4. **Myth: You Have to Change Everything at Once.**
   Sometimes, we feel we must overhaul our entire life to be better. But big changes can be overwhelming. Small steps are often more effective and easier to maintain. If you try to change your diet, your exercise habits, your sleep routine, your friendships, and your job all at once, you might get exhausted and quit. It's better to pick one or two areas to focus on first.
5. **Myth: Being Better Means You'll Never Fail.**
   Failure is a part of life. Even the most successful and wise people have failed many times. Improving yourself doesn't mean you won't fail. It means you learn from mistakes and keep going. In fact, mistakes can be our best teachers. They show us what not to do next time.

By understanding these myths, you can have a more realistic idea of what self-improvement looks like. You don't have to be perfect, and you don't have to do everything by yourself. The road to being better is filled with trial and error. You might try something and discover it doesn't work for you. That's okay. You simply try something else. As long as you keep learning and stay committed, you are moving in the right direction.

Section 4: The Difference Between "Being Better" and "Being Perfect"

Many people confuse the idea of "being better" with "being perfect." These are not the same. Perfection suggests there is a final state where we have no flaws, no struggles, and no room for growth. But in real life, no person is perfect. We all have limits, make mistakes, and deal with weaknesses.

When we talk about being better, we mean continuing to improve from where we are. We are not aiming to erase every flaw instantly. Instead, we aim to reduce the harmful effects of our flaws and build on our strengths. For instance, you might have a tendency to get angry when someone disagrees with you. If you work on it, you might still sometimes feel upset, but you learn to pause, breathe, and answer calmly more often. That is progress.

Focusing on perfection can be harmful because it sets an impossible standard. If you believe you must never make a mistake, you may become afraid to try new things. You might also feel awful whenever you fail at something, which can discourage you from trying again. In contrast, if your focus is on being better, each mistake becomes an opportunity to learn. You can look at what went wrong and try a new approach.

Moreover, seeking perfection can lead to stress and anxiety. It's normal to want to do well, but constantly worrying about being perfect can drain your energy. You might find yourself spending too much time trying to fix tiny details or fearing that others will judge you. This can make it hard to be happy with what you have accomplished.

In everyday life, you can see the difference between someone who wants to be better versus someone who wants to be perfect. The person who aims for better might set a goal to read 10 pages of a book every day. If one day they only read 5 pages, they still feel good about making some progress. But the person who wants to be perfect might insist on reading exactly 10 pages every single day without fail. If they read 9 pages one day, they might feel like a failure. This attitude can be harmful because it doesn't recognize that any effort is still a positive step.

Striving for improvement also means accepting that you're human. Humans learn in steps, and we all have different strengths and weaknesses. It's okay to celebrate small wins and be proud of yourself for trying. You don't have to compare yourself to others who might be better at some skill or further along in their personal journeys. Instead, compare yourself to who you were yesterday or last week or last year.

In short, do not aim for perfection. Aim for progress. Focus on the things you can control, do your best, and learn from whatever happens. This healthy mindset will help you enjoy the process more, and you'll likely see more real results in the long run.

Section 5: The Path of Lifelong Growth

Being better is not just for a specific age group or a specific time in your life. It is a journey that can last as long as you are alive. For example, a child can learn to be more patient with siblings or more careful with belongings. A teenager can learn to plan time better, study more effectively, or pick friends wisely. An adult might work on communication skills in relationships, learn how to manage money, or handle career changes. Even seniors can discover new hobbies, deepen family bonds, or volunteer to help others.

This idea of lifelong growth can be inspiring because it means you never have to stop learning or improving. You are not stuck in one place unless you decide to be. It can also be a relief to know that you do not have to rush to fix every flaw right now. You have your whole life to make small improvements, one after the other.

Sometimes people think that personal growth is only for people who are unhappy or struggling. But that is not true. Even if you are generally happy, you can still gain new skills or insights that make your life richer. For example, a happy person might still learn a new language, explore volunteer work, or improve public speaking skills. There is no limit to how far we can grow or how much we can learn.

It's also helpful to know that growth can happen in many areas. You might be focused on health and fitness at one point in your life, then shift to emotional well-being, then shift to social skills, and so on. Each area you work on can open the door to new opportunities and deeper satisfaction.

Lifelong growth also teaches us humility. No matter how much you learn or improve, there is always something else you can explore or do better. This humility is not meant to make you feel inferior. Instead, it keeps you open to learning from anyone and anything. You might learn from children, from peers, from elders, or even from the natural world. You start to see that the world is full of lessons if you pay attention.

One reason lifelong growth is so important is because life keeps changing. The world we live in is not the same world our grandparents lived in. And our children's world will be different from ours. If we do not keep growing, learning, and adapting, we might find ourselves stuck in old ways that no longer work. Growth helps us remain flexible and ready for whatever comes next.

Finally, the lifelong growth mindset encourages you to be patient with yourself. You understand that every skill takes time to develop and that mistakes are part of the process. If you have a bad day or make a mistake, you can remember that growth does not end in a single day. You can always begin again tomorrow. This patience and openness can make your journey much more enjoyable and fulfilling.

Section 6: Seeing the Whole Picture of Your Life

When we decide to be better, it's important to look at our lives in a balanced way. We are not just one thing—like a student, worker, or parent.

We are many things at once. We have physical health, mental health, emotional well-being, social relationships, financial concerns, and so on. If we focus on only one area and ignore the others, we might find ourselves unbalanced. For instance, if you spend all your time improving your career but never take care of your physical health, you might see success at work but feel exhausted or unwell. On the other hand, if you focus only on having fun and ignore your responsibilities, you might face problems with money or relationships down the line.

One way to see the whole picture is to take a moment and list the main areas of your life: health, family, friends, work or school, spirituality or beliefs (if that's important to you), hobbies, and community. Look at each area and ask yourself, "How am I doing here? What can I improve? How important is this area to me right now?" Some areas might need more attention than others, but it's good to ensure you're not neglecting anything important.

For example, you might realize that you've been so focused on getting good grades that you haven't spent much time with friends. Or maybe you've been so into your hobby that you're ignoring chores around the house. Balance doesn't mean you spend equal time on each area. It means you give each area enough attention so that you feel you are progressing in a well-rounded way.

It also helps to know which areas give you energy and which areas take energy from you. Some people feel energized after socializing, while others find it draining. Some people get a boost from exercise, while others prefer reading quietly. Knowing yourself helps you plan your time in a way that supports your growth without burning you out.

Keeping the whole picture in mind also helps you set goals that make sense. If you know you're lacking in the health department, you might focus on forming a consistent workout routine and healthier eating habits. If you realize you've been lonely, you might set a goal to join a club or reach out to friends more often. By looking at your life as a whole, you make sure you're improving in areas that truly matter to you.

This idea of balance doesn't mean you never work extra hard on one particular goal. Sometimes, life requires us to focus more on one area—like studying hard for an important exam or putting extra effort into a job project. But once that period is over, we should return to a more balanced approach. That way, we don't damage other important parts of our lives in the process.

Overall, seeing the whole picture reminds us that growth isn't just about one accomplishment. It's about living a better, more well-rounded life. When we are balanced, we feel stronger, clearer, and happier.

Section 7: Realistic Expectations and Patience

When you start working on being better, it can be tempting to expect quick changes. You might think, "I'll work on my habits for a week, and everything will be fixed." But real change takes time. It might take weeks, months, or even years to see the full effect of your efforts. That's why patience is so important.

It helps to set realistic expectations. For instance, if you want to lose weight or get fitter, you might start by exercising three times a week for 20 minutes. After a month, you might not see a huge transformation in the mirror, but you might notice you can climb stairs more easily or you have slightly more energy. Over time, these small improvements add up. If you expect to see big changes instantly, you might get discouraged and quit before you see real results.

Patience also means forgiving yourself when you slip up. If you have a goal to eat healthier and one day you end up eating a bunch of junk food, that doesn't mean you have failed completely. You can always start fresh the next day. The road to growth is rarely a straight line; it often has bumps, detours, and sometimes you even go backwards for a bit.

Another reason to keep realistic expectations is that life itself is unpredictable. You might have a plan to improve your finances by working extra hours, but then you or a family member gets sick. Or you might plan to run every morning but then break your ankle. These setbacks do not mean you are not improving. They just mean you have to adapt and find a new way. Perhaps you shift to doing gentle exercises while your ankle heals, or you find online work if you can't do your normal job.

Being patient helps you handle these twists and turns. Instead of feeling like you have to achieve everything right now, you learn to trust the process and keep moving forward when you can. Over the long run, this approach can bring far greater success than rushing and burning yourself out.

Finally, patience teaches us to enjoy the journey. Sometimes, people think they will only be happy once they reach their goal. But life is made up of daily moments, not just the final outcome. If you can find small joys and lessons in each step of the process, you will likely feel more motivated to continue. You might even find that the journey itself is more rewarding than the end result.

In summary, it's best to expect that growth will take time, that you might face setbacks, and that small steps do matter. Patience keeps you steady, helps you bounce back from mistakes, and teaches you to appreciate each stage of your progress.

Section 8: A Look at What's Ahead in This Book

In the next chapters, we will dive into specific areas of personal growth and practical ways to work on them. Here is a quick glance at what you can expect:

- **Understanding Your Starting Point:** You will learn how to honestly evaluate your current strengths and weaknesses, so you know where to begin your journey.
- **Setting Clear and Meaningful Goals:** This will help you create realistic targets that keep you motivated.
- **Building Self-Discipline:** We will talk about how to train your mind to stick to tasks, even when you don't feel like it.
- **Overcoming Fears and Doubts:** Fear can hold us back, but you can learn to face it in a healthy way.
- **Developing Healthy Habits:** Habits are powerful; forming good ones can make self-improvement much easier.
- **Growing Through Challenges and Failure:** Failure isn't the end; it can be a stepping stone if you learn from it.

- **Learning from Others:** Mentors, friends, and role models can help speed up your learning.
- **Nurturing Positive Relationships:** We'll look at how to communicate better, resolve conflicts, and build supportive relationships.
- **Managing Time and Energy:** Good time management helps you get more done without feeling overwhelmed.
- **Strengthening Self-Confidence:** Learn to believe in your abilities and worth.
- **Finding Motivation Every Day:** Daily motivation can be the difference between giving up and pushing on.
- **Being Responsible for Your Life:** Taking responsibility can make you feel empowered to create the changes you want.
- **Embracing Gratitude and Kindness:** We will see how gratitude and kindness can make both you and others happier.
- **Communicating Clearly and Respectfully:** Good communication solves many problems before they grow.
- **Facing Stress and Anxiety:** Learn healthy ways to handle pressure.
- **Balancing Work and Personal Life:** Keep all parts of your life in harmony.
- **Adapting to Change:** Change is inevitable; learning to handle it well can reduce anxiety.
- **Continuing Personal Growth Over a Lifetime:** Growth doesn't stop; there's always something new to learn.
- **Conclusion: A New Path Forward:** We'll wrap up everything and look at how you can keep going after you finish reading.

By the end of this book, you should have a solid toolbox of ideas and strategies to help you on your journey. Remember, you don't have to apply everything at once. Think of this book like a buffet. You can pick and choose the advice that fits your life right now. As you grow, you may come back to these chapters and find new meaning in them. That's the beauty of personal growth—it grows with you.

Chapter 2: Understanding Your Starting Point

Section 1: The Importance of Self-Reflection

Before you set out on any journey, it's good to know where you're starting from. In the context of personal growth, understanding your current self is crucial. Self-reflection is the tool that helps you look at your life honestly. It involves taking a step back from the noise of daily life and thinking about what's going well, what's not going well, and what you truly want.

Self-reflection can happen in many ways. Some people like to keep a journal where they write down their thoughts, feelings, and daily experiences. Others prefer to talk to a friend or counselor. Some might simply take a walk alone and think about their day or week. The key is to find a method that allows you to become aware of your inner world.

One benefit of self-reflection is that it helps you spot patterns in your behavior. For example, you might notice that you tend to lose your temper when you are hungry or tired. Or you might realize you get discouraged and quit whenever something feels too difficult. Seeing these patterns is the first step to changing them. If you don't know what your patterns are, you can't fix them.

Another benefit is that self-reflection helps you figure out your values and priorities. Sometimes, we think we want something because society or family tells us we should want it. But deep down, it may not be our true desire. By reflecting on your life, you might discover you'd rather have more free time than a high-paying job. Or you might realize that helping others is more important to you than climbing the career ladder. This clarity will guide you to set goals that make sense for you.

Self-reflection also encourages gratitude. When you look closely at your life, you might notice small blessings or improvements you previously overlooked. Maybe you have supportive friends, a roof over your head, or a skill that you've been taking for granted. Feeling grateful for what you already have can build a positive mindset that fuels further growth.

However, self-reflection also requires honesty. It can be uncomfortable to admit we have faults or that we made bad decisions. But facing these truths is necessary. If you pretend everything is fine when it isn't, you won't make meaningful changes. If you lie to yourself about your habits, you'll never move forward. In a way, being honest with yourself is one of the bravest things you can do, and it lays the foundation for genuine improvement.

In the end, self-reflection is a powerful tool that sets the stage for all other forms of growth. It helps you see your strengths, weaknesses, goals, and hopes. It puts you in a position to make better decisions about what you want to change or improve. Without it, you might end up chasing someone else's vision of success, which can lead to frustration and confusion. By starting with self-reflection, you begin your journey on solid ground.

Section 2: Identifying Strengths and Weaknesses

Once you start looking inward, you'll want to figure out your strengths and weaknesses. Strengths are the things you're naturally good at or have developed well over time. Weaknesses are areas where you struggle or lack certain skills. Everyone has both, and recognizing them can help you decide where to focus your energy.

Why Strengths Matter

Your strengths can be your foundation. They are the things that make you feel capable, confident, and unique. Some common strengths include good communication skills, empathy, creativity, problem-solving ability, or leadership qualities. By identifying your strengths, you can use them to reach your goals faster. For example, if you are good at organizing tasks, you can use that skill to structure your day efficiently.

Why Weaknesses Matter

Weaknesses are not something to be ashamed of. They are simply signals telling you where you might need to learn or grow. Some examples of weaknesses could be fear of public speaking, poor time management, lack of patience, or avoiding difficult conversations. By identifying these areas, you can work on them directly. That might mean taking a course, practicing new habits, or seeking help from someone with more experience.

Finding Your Strengths and Weaknesses

You can try different methods to figure out what you're good at and where you need improvement:

1. **Journaling:** Write down the tasks you do in a day or a week. Note which ones feel easy or enjoyable and which ones you dread or mess up.
2. **Asking Others:** Sometimes friends, family, or colleagues see things in us that we don't see in ourselves. You can ask them what they think your strongest qualities are and what you might want to work on.
3. **Reflection on Successes and Failures:** Think about past successes. What qualities or skills helped you succeed? Then look at times you failed. What caused the failure? Was there a lack of knowledge or a particular habit that led to the outcome?
4. **Personality or Skills Assessments:** There are many online tools or professional assessments that can give you insights into your personality traits, skills, and potential blind spots.

Balancing Growth

Once you know your strengths and weaknesses, you can make a plan to build on the good stuff and work on the not-so-good stuff. But remember, you don't have to turn every weakness into a strength. Some weaknesses might not be that important in the grand scheme of your life. If you have a weakness that seriously holds you back—like an inability to communicate well or manage money—then it's worth putting in the time to improve it.

At the same time, don't ignore your strengths. Improving yourself doesn't mean only fixing what's wrong. It also means becoming even better at what you're already good at. This can lead to greater enjoyment, success, and fulfillment. For example, if you're good at art, you might take classes to refine your technique or explore new mediums.

Finally, remember that strengths and weaknesses can change over time. As you gain new experiences, you might develop skills in areas you used to struggle with. You may also find that some strengths fade if you don't use them. Staying aware of this helps you adapt and keep growing throughout your life.

Section 3: Understanding Your Emotional Landscape

Your emotional landscape is the range of feelings you experience on a regular basis. Emotions play a big role in how you live your life, how you see yourself, and how you interact with others. If you ignore your emotions, you might find yourself acting in ways you don't fully understand.

Common Emotions and Their Purpose

Humans experience many emotions: happiness, sadness, anger, fear, surprise, and disgust, among others. Each emotion serves a purpose. For instance, fear can keep you alert and safe from dangers, while happiness encourages you to repeat enjoyable experiences. Anger can signal that you feel something is unfair or that your boundaries have been crossed.

Emotional Triggers

A trigger is something that causes a strong emotional reaction. It could be a memory, a word someone says, a situation, or even a certain smell. By identifying your triggers, you gain control over how you respond to them. Instead of getting swept away by anger or anxiety, you can pause, take a deep breath, and decide on a healthier response.

Dealing With Negative Emotions

Negative emotions like sadness, anger, or fear are not bad in themselves. They become harmful when we let them control us or when we don't know how to handle them. For example, feeling sad sometimes is natural and can help us process loss. But if sadness lingers for too long without proper care, it might lead to depression. Similarly, anger can be a useful signal that something is wrong, but uncontrolled anger can damage relationships.

Building Emotional Awareness

One way to build emotional awareness is to practice naming your emotions. When you feel something, try to identify the emotion as specifically as possible—"I'm feeling disappointed," "I'm feeling frustrated," or "I'm feeling anxious." This simple act of naming can give you a moment to reflect instead of reacting automatically. Another helpful habit is checking in with yourself throughout the day: "What am I feeling right now?" If you're stressed, ask yourself why. Is it because of a deadline, an argument, or too many responsibilities?

Emotional Balance

Part of understanding your starting point is seeing if your emotions are balanced. Do you find yourself overwhelmed by negative emotions often? Or are you generally calm and content? Neither state is permanent, but noticing the pattern can guide you in deciding what to work on. If you notice that you're often anxious, maybe you can learn some relaxation techniques or talk to a therapist. If you notice you're often angry, maybe you can explore conflict resolution strategies or anger management tools.

Being in tune with your emotional landscape can also improve your relationships. When you understand what you're feeling and why, you can express yourself more clearly. Instead of snapping at someone, you can calmly explain that you feel stressed or upset. This helps reduce misunderstandings and builds trust with those around you.

Emotions are a key part of being human. They can enrich your life or cause problems, depending on how you deal with them. By examining and understanding your emotions, you set a strong foundation for every other change or goal you might pursue.

Section 4: Assessing Your Mindset

Your mindset is the lens through which you see the world. It shapes your beliefs about yourself and your abilities. Generally, people talk about two main types of mindset: fixed mindset and growth mindset.

Fixed Mindset

A person with a fixed mindset believes that their traits—intelligence, skills, and talents—are mostly unchangeable. They think people are born with certain abilities, and there's not much you can do to improve. If you have a fixed mindset, you might avoid challenges because you fear failure. You might take feedback personally and feel threatened by the success of others.

Growth Mindset

A person with a growth mindset believes that intelligence, skills, and talents can be developed through hard work, good strategies, and help from others. If you have a growth mindset, you see challenges as opportunities to learn. You welcome feedback because it helps you improve, and you feel inspired (rather than threatened) by the achievements of other people.

Why Mindset Matters

If you have a fixed mindset, you might hold yourself back from trying new things because you believe you can't get better. You might also give up easily when you face obstacles. On the other hand, a growth mindset encourages you to keep going, learn from mistakes, and view setbacks as part of the process. It's a powerful shift that can improve how you handle life's ups and downs.

Checking Your Own Mindset

To see which mindset you lean toward, pay attention to your self-talk. If you often say, "I'm just not good at this," or "I'll never understand this," you might be showing signs of a fixed mindset. If you find yourself thinking, "I can get better at this if I practice," or "I need to try a different approach," you're leaning more toward a growth mindset.

You might also have a mixed mindset, where you believe you can grow in some areas but not in others. For instance, you might believe you can improve your cooking skills but think your math abilities are fixed. Recognizing where you have a fixed view can help you work on shifting it to a growth view.

Changing Your Mindset

You can train your mind to be more growth-oriented. One approach is to reframe your thoughts. Instead of saying, "I can't do this," add the word "yet" to the end: "I can't do this yet." This subtle change acknowledges that improvement is possible in the future. Another approach is to see effort as a sign of progress, not weakness. When you struggle with a task, remind yourself that the struggle is part of learning. Praise yourself for hard work rather than just outcomes.

Practical Steps

- **Embrace Challenges:** Try something new or difficult, knowing you might not be good at it right away.
- **Learn from Criticism:** When someone gives you feedback, thank them. Ask how you can improve instead of feeling attacked.
- **Celebrate Others' Success:** If someone does well, see it as proof that you can achieve your goals too, rather than feeling jealous.
- **Focus on Process Over Results:** Keep track of how you're learning and what strategies you're using, not just the final score or grade.

By checking your mindset and making it more growth-focused, you set the stage for all the improvements you want to make in your life. It might feel strange at first if you're used to thinking of yourself as fixed. But with practice, you can develop a mindset that believes in the possibility of change.

Section 5: Taking Stock of Your Environment

Your environment includes your home, school, workplace, the people around you, and even the cultural or social context you live in. This environment can have a big impact on your personal growth. For example, if you live in a supportive home, you might find it easier to stick to good habits. If you have negative influences around you, you might struggle with stress or unhealthy behaviors.

Taking stock of your environment means asking these questions:

1. **Who Are the People Around Me?**
   Do they encourage you, or do they bring you down? Do they listen to you, or do they ignore you? Are they working on their own growth, or are they stuck in negativity?
2. **Physical Space:**
   Is your living or working area cluttered or organized? Does it help you focus or distract you? For instance, if you want to study or work on a project, having a clean, quiet space can help you concentrate.
3. **Online Environment:**
   In today's world, we spend a lot of time online. The websites you visit, the social media accounts you follow, and the type of news you consume can affect your mindset. If you're always reading negative, scary news, you might feel more anxious. If you follow uplifting, educational content, you might feel more motivated and informed.
4. **Community and Culture:**
   The larger community you belong to (school, neighborhood, city, or even your nation) also has an impact. Some communities value collaboration, creativity, and learning. Others might be more

competitive, stressful, or even unsafe. This environment can shape how you think about yourself and your goals.

Understanding your environment allows you to make changes. For example, if you realize your home is too noisy for you to focus, you might find a library or a quiet café to work in. If you see that certain friends always discourage you, you might decide to spend less time with them and more time with people who support your goals. If you notice that being on social media too much makes you feel bad about yourself, you might limit your usage or follow accounts that uplift you.

Sometimes, you can't change certain aspects of your environment—maybe you can't move houses right now or switch schools immediately. In that case, you can look for small changes that help. You might keep your personal room tidy or put up motivational quotes. You could also wear headphones to reduce noise or schedule your study time when the house is calmer.

If your environment is really challenging—like if you live in a dangerous area or face ongoing discrimination—it's important to acknowledge that those challenges are real. You might need extra support, such as counseling, community resources, or a mentor who understands your situation. You're not failing if you need help; you're simply adapting to tough circumstances.

Overall, your environment matters because it can either push you forward or hold you back. By taking stock of it, you empower yourself to make changes—big or small—that can help you grow more effectively.

Section 6: Clarifying What You Want

Now that you've spent some time thinking about your internal state—your emotions, mindset, and strengths—as well as your external environment, it's time to clarify what you truly want out of life. This step goes beyond just setting goals. It's about understanding your desires, values, and the vision you have for your future.

Long-Term Vision

A long-term vision is like a distant lighthouse guiding your journey. It might be something broad, such as "I want to be healthy, happy, and make a positive impact on the world." Or it might be more specific, like "I want to become a teacher and help children learn." Your vision doesn't have to be perfect or unchangeable. It's a starting point that can evolve over time. What matters is that it gives you direction and motivation.

Short-Term Goals

Once you have a sense of your long-term vision, break it down into smaller, short-term goals. For example, if your vision is to be healthier, a short-term goal might be "walk for 20 minutes every day" or "eat vegetables with at least one meal per day." If your vision is to be a teacher, a short-term goal could be "research teaching degree programs" or "volunteer at a local tutoring center."

Values and Priorities

Sometimes, we set goals that don't align with our values or priorities. For instance, you might set a goal to make more money but realize that you actually value free time with family more than a higher salary. Clarifying your values can help you avoid chasing the wrong things. Think about what matters most to you: family, friendship, creativity, learning, helping others, independence, or adventure. Then, let those values guide your decisions.

Check for Realism

As you identify what you want, it's wise to check if your desires are realistic, at least in the short term. If you suddenly say, "I want to become a world-famous singer," but you've never sung before, that goal might be too big to start with. A more realistic initial goal could be, "I will take singing lessons and perform at local events." By being realistic, you set yourself up for success and avoid quick disappointment.

Flexibility

It's also important to remain flexible. Sometimes, as you pursue a goal, you learn more about yourself or the world, and your desires change. Maybe you discover you love something else even more, or maybe your life situation changes. Being flexible with your wants and goals can save you from frustration.

The Power of Clarity

When you know what you want, it becomes easier to say "no" to things that don't move you toward that vision. Clarity makes it easier to stay motivated because you have a reason behind your actions. It also helps you measure your progress: if your goal is to learn guitar, you can track how many chords you master or how many songs you can play.

In short, clarifying what you want is about aligning your deeper values with your daily actions and long-term plans. This clarity not only guides your growth but also brings a sense of purpose to your life.

Section 7: Creating a Personal Inventory

After exploring your emotions, mindset, strengths, weaknesses, environment, and desires, you might find it helpful to create a personal inventory. This is a written (or typed) snapshot of who you are at this point in your life. It can include the following sections:

1. **Strengths:** List at least five things you do well or qualities you're proud of.
2. **Weaknesses:** List areas you'd like to improve.
3. **Values:** Note the principles that guide your life (like honesty, compassion, growth, or adventure).
4. **Interests:** Write down activities or topics you enjoy.
5. **Goals:** Short-term goals and long-term goals you'd like to achieve.
6. **Environmental Factors:** Positive or negative influences in your home, work, or community.

7. **Mindset Reflection:** A brief note on whether you think you have a fixed mindset or a growth mindset in different areas.
8. **Emotional Patterns:** Key emotions you feel often and possible triggers.

You can update this personal inventory every few months or once a year to see how you're progressing. It can serve as a reminder of where you started and what you wanted to work on. You might be surprised to see how much you can change when you look back a year later.

The personal inventory is not about labeling yourself as "good" or "bad." It's about having a clear picture. When you know what you're dealing with, you can come up with a plan that makes sense. For instance, if you see that you value "kindness" but often get into arguments, you might decide to practice listening skills. If you notice you're always tired and realize your environment is noisy at night, you might look for ways to improve your sleep setup.

Keeping your personal inventory in a private place can also allow you to be completely honest. You don't have to worry about what anyone else thinks. This honesty is vital for real growth. After all, change starts with understanding where you really are.

Section 8: Setting the Stage for Change

Now that you have a better understanding of yourself, you are in a great position to start making changes. Here's how you can set the stage for success:

1. **Pick a Focus Area:** Instead of trying to change everything at once, choose one area of your life you'd like to improve first. It could be health, relationships, mindset, or career.
2. **Set Simple, Clear Goals:** Aim for goals that are specific and measurable. For example, if you want better health, a clear goal might be "I will walk 30 minutes each day for 5 days a week."
3. **Create a Support System:** Let friends or family know about your goals. If they understand what you're trying to do, they can help

you stay accountable. Or, join a group of people who have similar goals.
4. **Plan for Obstacles:** Life is full of surprises. Think about what might go wrong (like getting busy at work) and come up with a plan to keep going anyway.
5. **Start Small:** It's tempting to make grand plans, but small actions done consistently often lead to bigger results over time.
6. **Track Your Progress:** Keep a record of what you do each day or week. Tracking can motivate you and show you if you need to adjust your plan.
7. **Celebrate Milestones:** When you reach a small milestone, treat yourself to something you enjoy. This keeps your spirits high and makes the process more fun.

These steps help you transition from simply understanding yourself to actively changing your life. The more prepared you are, the more likely you'll handle setbacks calmly and keep moving forward.

Chapter 3: Setting Clear and Meaningful Goals

Introduction

In the first two chapters, we explored the importance of knowing where you stand right now—your strengths, weaknesses, emotions, mindset, and environment. Now, it's time to use that self-knowledge to set clear and meaningful goals. Goals give you direction. They keep you focused on what matters and remind you why you're putting in effort. Without goals, it's easy to drift through life, doing whatever comes your way without a sense of purpose.

In this chapter, we will learn how to create goals that match your values, fit your current abilities, and still push you to grow. We will talk about how to make goals specific and doable, so you don't feel lost or overwhelmed. You'll learn strategies for staying on track, measuring your progress, and overcoming common obstacles. By the end of this chapter, you will have the tools you need to turn your dreams and ideas into clear targets you can work toward every day. Setting good goals isn't just about writing words on paper; it's about understanding what truly matters to you, then crafting a plan to get there step by step.

Section 1: Why Goals Matter

Goals give structure and meaning to our actions. Imagine waking up each day with no plan, no purpose, and no idea what you want to accomplish. You might go through the motions—eating, going to school or work, returning home—without ever feeling like you made progress in your life. Goals change that. They act like a signpost that reminds you, "This is where I'm heading."

Direction and Focus

One of the main reasons goals matter is that they help you focus your time and energy. We all have 24 hours in a day, but how we use those hours differs depending on whether we have goals. A person with a goal to get healthier might decide to spend an hour walking or exercising. A person without goals might just watch TV or scroll on social media. Goals help you make choices that align with your priorities.

Sense of Achievement

Goals also give you a sense of achievement. When you set a goal and reach it, you feel proud of yourself. That feeling can motivate you to set and achieve more goals. Even small wins—like finishing a book, learning a new recipe, or saving a little money—can inspire you to keep going. Over time, these small achievements add up and boost your confidence.

Measuring Progress

Another benefit of goals is that they let you measure your progress. If your goal is to run a certain distance without stopping, you can track how far you run each week. You might start at a short distance, but over the weeks, you'll see your stamina improving. This visual proof can be very motivating. It shows you that your efforts are making a difference.

Overcoming Distractions

In our busy world, it's easy to get distracted by countless activities. From social media to video games to online shopping, there's always something competing for our attention. Goals act like a filter. When you know what you want—like improving your grades, learning a new language, or getting fit—you are more likely to say "no" to time-wasting activities. Instead, you focus on what gets you closer to your goal.

Building Discipline

Finally, having clear goals helps build discipline. Discipline is the ability to stick with something even when you don't feel like it. When you have a strong reason behind your actions—such as a goal you're excited about—it's easier to push past laziness or boredom. For example, if your goal is to finish a writing project, you might write every day, even on days you feel tired. The goal reminds you why you started in the first place.

In short, goals matter because they give you a roadmap for how to spend your time and energy. They provide direction, focus, and a sense of accomplishment. They help you measure how far you've come and remind you to keep going when life gets tough or distracting. Whether your goals are big or small, having them is a key part of making steady progress and leading a meaningful life.

Section 2: Types of Goals – Short-Term vs. Long-Term

Not all goals are the same. Some you can achieve in a few days or weeks, while others might take years. It's helpful to understand the difference between short-term and long-term goals, because both play important roles in your growth.

Short-Term Goals

Short-term goals are objectives you can reach in a relatively short period. This could be anywhere from a day to a few months. Examples include:

- Finishing a book in two weeks.
- Saving a small amount of money this month.
- Going for a daily walk for one month.
- Improving a specific skill at work or school over the next few weeks.

Short-term goals are great for building momentum and confidence. Because they're more immediate, you get to see results sooner. This boosts your motivation to tackle bigger challenges. Think of short-term goals as stepping stones. Each small success encourages you to aim higher and keep moving forward.

Long-Term Goals

Long-term goals usually take many months or even years to achieve. Examples might be:

- Completing a college degree.
- Mastering a new language well enough to hold long conversations.
- Building a successful business.
- Saving for a down payment on a house.
- Improving your athletic skills to a competition level.

These goals require patience, persistence, and a clear plan. They also provide a sense of direction for your life. For instance, if your long-term goal is to become a teacher, you know you'll need to go to college, get certain qualifications, and possibly do student teaching. Each step on that path can be broken down into smaller short-term goals—like researching schools, applying for scholarships, or finishing each semester successfully.

Balancing Both

You might wonder how to balance short-term and long-term goals. The key is to ensure they complement each other. For instance, if your long-term goal is to learn a new language, your short-term goals might include learning five new vocabulary words every day, listening to language podcasts twice a week, or completing a beginner-level course in three months. Each short-term goal is a piece of the puzzle that helps you reach the big picture.

Flexibility in Goals

It's also important to be flexible. Sometimes, as you work on a long-term goal, you discover new interests or face life changes that lead you to adjust or even change your goal. That's okay. Goals aren't meant to lock you into one path forever. They're meant to guide you as you grow and learn more about yourself and the world. If your situation changes, it can be wise to revisit your goals and see if they still fit your current needs and desires.

In summary, having both short-term and long-term goals is beneficial. Short-term goals give you quick wins and keep you motivated day to day.

Long-term goals provide the bigger vision and purpose that remind you why you're making the effort. By balancing both, you create a solid structure for steady, meaningful progress.

Section 3: The Qualities of Effective Goals

Now that we've talked about why goals matter and the difference between short-term and long-term goals, let's look at what makes a goal truly effective. You've probably heard about the concept of "SMART" goals. It's a simple way to remember the qualities a goal should have to be successful. While different people sometimes use different words for each letter, here's one common interpretation:

1. **S – Specific**
   A specific goal answers "who, what, where, why, and how." Instead of saying, "I want to be healthy," you might say, "I will walk for 30 minutes every day in my neighborhood to improve my cardiovascular health." The more specific you are, the clearer your path becomes.
2. **M – Measurable**
   If you can't measure a goal, you won't know when you achieve it. For instance, "Eat better" is vague. Instead, you could measure it by "Eating at least one serving of vegetables with each meal" or "Limiting sugary drinks to two per week." Measurable goals let you track progress and celebrate milestones.
3. **A – Achievable**
   Your goal should be realistic and attainable given your current resources and abilities. Setting a goal to run a marathon in two weeks when you've never run before is likely too big a leap. Aim for something that challenges you but isn't impossible. Otherwise, you risk frustration and burnout.
4. **R – Relevant**
   A relevant goal aligns with your values, interests, and life situation. If you have no real interest in a particular skill, there's little reason to work toward it. Make sure your goals matter to you personally;

this emotional connection keeps you motivated when things get tough.
5. **T – Time-Bound**
   A deadline gives you a sense of urgency. Instead of saying, "I want to learn a new programming language someday," say, "I want to learn the basics of this programming language within the next three months." Having an end date pushes you to schedule your steps and avoid procrastination.

Example of a SMART Goal

Let's say you want to improve your public speaking. A SMART goal might be:

- **Specific:** "I will join my local public speaking club to practice making speeches in front of an audience."
- **Measurable:** "I will give one short speech every two weeks at the club."
- **Achievable:** "I have time to attend the club meetings twice a month, and I can practice at home."
- **Relevant:** "I want to improve my communication skills for my future career."
- **Time-Bound:** "I plan to do this for three months and see if I have gained more confidence by then."

By making the goal SMART, you have a clear roadmap. You know exactly what you're doing, why you're doing it, when, and how to measure success.

Staying Flexible

Remember that even SMART goals might need adjusting. If you find the goal is too easy, you can raise the bar. If it's too hard, you can scale it down. The point is to keep it both challenging and realistic so you don't lose motivation.

Section 4: Breaking Down Big Goals

Large goals can be exciting but also intimidating. If your goal is to write a book, you might feel overwhelmed just thinking about how much work goes into it. This is why **breaking down big goals into smaller steps** is crucial. It makes the path clearer and less scary. Instead of jumping straight to "write a book," you might start with smaller tasks like brainstorming ideas, outlining chapters, or writing a page each day.

Chunking Your Goal

The process of breaking down a goal into small parts is often called "chunking." For example, if your big goal is to run a half marathon (about 21 kilometers), you can chunk it into:

1. **Research a Training Plan:** Spend a week or two learning about half-marathon training schedules.
2. **Start Running Short Distances:** Aim for 1–2 kilometers at a comfortable pace.
3. **Increase Distance Gradually:** Every week, add a bit more distance to your runs.
4. **Include Rest and Cross-Training:** Plan days for stretching, weight training, or yoga.
5. **Track Progress Weekly:** Keep a simple log of each run—distance, pace, how you felt.

By dividing the big goal into smaller tasks, each task feels more achievable. You're not stressing about running 21 kilometers on day one. You're focusing on learning and making steady progress.

Setting Milestones

Once you chunk your goal, set milestones to mark key points in your journey. A milestone is like a checkpoint. Going back to the half-marathon example, your first milestone might be running 5 kilometers without stopping. Your second milestone might be running 10 kilometers, and so on. Each milestone is something to celebrate because it shows how far you've come. Celebrations can be simple: maybe you treat yourself to a healthy snack, buy a new running shirt, or share your achievement with supportive friends. Recognizing milestones keeps you motivated for the next one.

Adjusting as You Go

Sometimes, as you work on the smaller tasks, you discover you need more time or you can handle more than you thought. This is normal. Goals aren't meant to be rigid. Feel free to adjust your schedule or your tasks as you learn what works best for you. If you get sick for a week and miss some training, extend your timeline or reduce your daily run until you're healthy again. The key is to keep moving forward, even if you have to go a bit slower or change the plan.

Avoiding Burnout

Breaking down big goals also helps prevent burnout. If you try to take on too much at once, you could exhaust yourself mentally or physically, leading you to quit. Smaller, manageable tasks protect you from that risk. They let you keep a steady pace. You can monitor how you're feeling and pause if you need rest.

Practical Tips

- Use a planner or a digital app to list your smaller tasks and check them off as you complete them.
- Share your plan with a friend or mentor who can support you.
- Reflect on each step you finish: what went well, what could improve, and how you felt.
- Remember that small consistent actions often lead to big results over time.

Breaking down big goals turns a daunting project into a series of manageable steps. This approach not only keeps your motivation high but also allows you to adapt and learn along the way.

Section 5: Overcoming Goal-Setting Challenges

While setting goals can be exciting, it's not always easy. You might face doubt, fear, or even external obstacles. Here are common challenges people face when setting goals and how to overcome them:

1. **Lack of Clarity**
   Sometimes, you might feel you want to achieve something but can't quite name it. This lack of clarity can stall your progress. A good way to tackle this is by brainstorming. Write down anything that comes to mind, even if it sounds silly. Eventually, patterns may emerge, helping you find a clear direction.
2. **Fear of Failure**
   Many people avoid setting ambitious goals because they're afraid they won't succeed. One way to handle this fear is to remind yourself that failure is not the end. It's part of the learning process. You could also set smaller goals at first so you can see progress and build confidence.
3. **Overly Ambitious Goals**
   Setting goals that are too big can lead to burnout. If you find yourself getting overwhelmed, try scaling back. Make your goal more realistic, or break it down into smaller tasks. You can always increase the challenge once you've mastered the basics.
4. **Procrastination**
   Even with a clear goal, it's easy to put things off. To combat procrastination, create a schedule or routine. For instance, if your goal is to practice an instrument, set aside a specific time each day for practice. Keep your practice sessions short at first so they don't feel daunting. Over time, you can extend them.
5. **Inconsistent Motivation**
   Motivation naturally rises and falls. On some days, you'll feel full of energy. On others, you might not want to do anything. That's normal. When motivation is low, rely on discipline and the routines you've built. Also, revisit the reasons you set your goal in the first place—maybe write those reasons down somewhere visible so you can remind yourself why this goal matters.

6. **External Obstacles**
   Sometimes, outside factors like financial issues, lack of time, or family responsibilities can get in the way. When faced with these constraints, look for creative solutions. If money is tight, see if there's a free or low-cost way to work toward your goal. If time is limited, maybe wake up 30 minutes earlier a few days a week or organize your tasks more efficiently.
7. **Negative Influences**
   Some people around you may not support your goals. They may say you can't do it or think it's a waste of time. While you can't control what others say, you can control how you respond. Try to surround yourself with people who lift you up or join groups that share similar aspirations. Seek out mentors who have walked the path you want to walk.

Staying Committed

No matter the challenge, staying committed to your goals is crucial. Commitment doesn't mean you never feel uncertain or tired. It means you keep going because you remember what you want to achieve and why. You might tweak your timeline or approach, but you don't give up on your overall purpose.

Section 6: Tracking Progress and Celebrating Wins

Reaching your goals doesn't happen overnight. It's a journey, and along the way, it helps to track your progress and celebrate milestones. Tracking shows you where you've improved and where you might need to adjust your approach. Celebrating keeps you motivated by reminding you how far you've come.

Methods of Tracking

- **Journaling:** Write down daily or weekly notes on what you did to move closer to your goal. You can also note how you felt, any challenges you faced, and what you plan to do next.
- **Checklists or Spreadsheets:** For more detailed tracking, use a spreadsheet where you record data points, like how many pages you wrote, how many minutes you exercised, or how much money you saved. Checking off items can be satisfying and keep you organized.
- **Apps and Digital Tools:** Many free apps help you set goals and track habits. They often include reminders, charts, and motivational messages. Pick an app that suits your style and makes it easy for you to log progress.

Reviewing Regularly

Make time to review your progress, whether it's daily, weekly, or monthly. This review helps you see if you're on track. If you notice that you're behind on your tasks, figure out why. Are you facing an unexpected obstacle? Did you set the goal too high? Do you need more support? Reviewing and adjusting is normal and healthy; it prevents you from feeling stuck.

Positive Reinforcement

Celebrating wins is an important part of the goal-setting process. Positive reinforcement is when you reward yourself for doing the right thing. This could be something small, like enjoying a piece of your favorite fruit, or something bigger, like going to a movie or buying a new book. These rewards don't have to be expensive or grand. The point is to create a positive link in your mind between effort and feeling good.

Sharing Achievements

It can also be motivating to share your accomplishments with supportive friends or family members. Telling someone, "I just hit my target for the week!" can feel great, especially if they cheer you on or congratulate you. Online communities can also provide encouragement and ideas. But be careful about who you share your goals with—only share with people who can genuinely support you or provide constructive feedback.

Staying Humble

While celebrating is important, it's also wise to stay humble and remember you're still on a journey. Celebrating doesn't mean you become complacent. Instead, it's a way to recognize your effort while maintaining the drive to continue. If you ever feel tempted to slack off after a success, remind yourself that true growth is an ongoing process.

Building Momentum

When you track progress and celebrate along the way, you build momentum. Each small win makes it easier to tackle the next challenge. Over time, these successes stack up, boosting your confidence and skill set. You may even surprise yourself at how much you can achieve when you maintain a steady, focused approach.

Section 7: Real-Life Goal-Setting Examples

Sometimes it's helpful to see how goal-setting works in real life. Below are a few scenarios to illustrate different ways people set and achieve goals.

Example 1: A Student Improving Grades

- **Situation:** Alex is in high school and has been getting low grades in math.
- **Goal:** Raise math grade from a C to a B by the end of the semester.
- **Action Plan:**
    1. Ask the teacher for extra help or clarification once a week.
    2. Spend 30 minutes daily practicing math problems.
    3. Join a study group with classmates.
- **Tracking:** Keep a log of daily practice and note test scores to see improvement.

- **Celebration:** If Alex sees improvement on each test, they treat themselves to their favorite snack.

Example 2: An Adult Seeking Better Health

- **Situation:** Dana works full-time and feels tired all the time due to poor eating habits and no exercise.
- **Goal:** Improve fitness and lose 10 pounds in three months.
- **Action Plan:**
    1. Go for a 20-minute walk four times a week.
    2. Replace soda with water or tea.
    3. Prep meals on Sundays to avoid fast food during the week.
- **Tracking:** Use a simple spreadsheet to note daily activity and weight changes each week.
- **Celebration:** For every 5 pounds lost, buy a small but meaningful gift (like a new workout shirt).

Example 3: A Worker Wanting a Promotion

- **Situation:** Jin wants to move up at the company but lacks certain leadership skills.
- **Goal:** Improve leadership skills and apply for a managerial position within six months.
- **Action Plan:**
    1. Read one leadership book each month.
    2. Take an online course about management.
    3. Volunteer to lead small team projects at work to gain experience.
- **Tracking:** Keep notes about each project and the lessons learned, gather feedback from colleagues.
- **Celebration:** Treat yourself to a nice dinner or a weekend getaway if you complete the online course and get positive feedback from your boss.

In each example, the person has a clear target and a plan broken down into small steps. They also have a way to track their progress and a reward system that keeps them motivated. These examples show that goal-setting can be adapted to different ages, lifestyles, and challenges.

Section 8: Keeping Goals Aligned with Personal Values

It's possible to set goals that don't truly match who you are or what you value. You might do this because of peer pressure, family expectations, or social media influences. For example, if you're not interested in being famous but all your friends are talking about it, you might feel forced to set a goal that doesn't really fit you. This can lead to frustration or a sense of emptiness even if you reach the goal.

Identifying Your Values

Your values are the principles that guide your life. Common values include honesty, family, respect, health, learning, creativity, and kindness. If you're not sure what your values are, think about times when you felt proud of yourself or extremely satisfied. Chances are, you were acting in line with an important value. For example, if you felt great after helping a friend, maybe kindness or service is a value you hold dear.

Matching Goals to Values

When setting a goal, ask yourself, "Is this goal something that will honor my values?" For instance, if health is a major value for you, setting a goal to improve your diet or exercise routine makes sense. If creativity is a value, maybe you want to set a goal to learn painting or compose music. When your goals line up with your values, it's easier to stay motivated because you feel you're doing something that truly matters to you.

Avoiding Comparison

One problem in modern life is the tendency to compare ourselves to others. If you see someone on social media who seems to have a perfect life, you might set a goal just to keep up with them. But that person's goals might be driven by their own values, which may not match yours. Instead of copying someone else's path, focus on what brings you joy and fulfillment.

Adjusting Goals When Values Shift

Values can change or grow as you experience different stages of life. Maybe you once valued adventure above all else, but now family has become more important. In that case, your goals might shift from traveling the world to building a stable home environment. This shift isn't a failure; it's an adaptation to your changing self. Allow yourself to reevaluate your goals when you sense your values have evolved.

Staying True to Yourself

Keeping your goals aligned with your values helps you stay true to yourself. When you act in ways that match your deepest beliefs, you often experience greater happiness and peace of mind. Even if the journey is tough, you'll feel a sense of purpose because you're moving in a direction that genuinely resonates with you.

In the end, goals are tools. They serve you, not the other way around. If a goal no longer fits who you are, it's completely acceptable to adjust or replace it. This is all part of the natural growth process.

Section 9: Practical Goal-Setting Tips

To wrap up this chapter on setting clear and meaningful goals, here are some practical tips you can start using right away:

1. **Start Small**
   If goal-setting feels overwhelming, pick just one small goal to work on first. Achieving even a tiny goal can give you the boost you need to tackle bigger ones later.
2. **Write It Down**
   Whether you use a notebook or a digital app, writing your goals down makes them feel more real. It also gives you something to revisit when you need a reminder of what you're aiming for.
3. **Share Selectively**
   Telling supportive friends or family about your goals can keep you

accountable. However, be mindful of sharing with people who might discourage or criticize you. Choose your support circle wisely.

4. **Set a Deadline**
   Even if it's just a rough timeline, having a target date can push you to take action instead of putting things off. Remember to be realistic with your deadline so you don't add unnecessary stress.

5. **Visualize Success**
   Spend a few minutes each day picturing yourself achieving your goal. This mental practice can help strengthen your belief in your ability to succeed and keep you motivated.

6. **Check In Regularly**
   Schedule a weekly or monthly review to see how you're doing. Ask yourself: What went well? What was challenging? What's the next step? Adjust your plan if necessary.

7. **Learn From Others**
   Seek out people who have accomplished what you want to achieve. Learn from their experiences, mistakes, and advice. You might find tips or shortcuts that apply to your situation.

8. **Focus on the Next Step**
   When the big goal feels overwhelming, focus on just the next step. You don't have to figure out every detail at once. Just keep taking one step forward, then another.

9. **Celebrate and Reflect**
   Every time you reach a milestone or a mini-goal, take a moment to celebrate. Reflect on what helped you succeed and how you can apply those lessons to the next step.

10. **Stay Adaptable**
    Life isn't static. Goals can change. Situations can shift. Keep an open mind and don't be afraid to update your plan when you need to.

By applying these tips, you'll be better equipped to set goals that are both meaningful and achievable. You'll also learn how to keep going when your motivation dips or when unexpected obstacles arise.

Chapter 4: Building Self-Discipline

Introduction

Having clear goals is only half the battle. The other half is the ability to follow through on those goals, especially when you don't feel like it. That's where self-discipline comes in. Self-discipline is the power to do what needs to be done—even when you're tired, bored, or tempted by distractions. It's what keeps you studying for an exam instead of binge-watching your favorite show, or sticking to your budget instead of spending money on unnecessary items.

In this chapter, we will explore how to develop and strengthen self-discipline. We'll talk about the habits and thought patterns that help you stay on track. We'll also discuss practical strategies for overcoming procrastination, dealing with setbacks, and managing temptations. By the end, you'll see that self-discipline is not about being perfect or punishing yourself. It's about respecting your own goals and making consistent choices that lead you closer to success.

Section 1: Understanding Self-Discipline

What Is Self-Discipline?

Self-discipline is the ability to regulate your own actions and behaviors to achieve desired outcomes. It involves controlling impulses and delaying instant gratification. Instead of looking for the easiest or most fun option right now, self-discipline helps you choose what will benefit you in the long run.

Why It Matters

Without self-discipline, even the best goals or dreams can fall apart. For instance, you might know that studying every night helps you understand the material better. But if you lack discipline, you may skip study sessions repeatedly. Over time, those small missed sessions add up, and you find yourself unprepared for exams.

Self-discipline affects many areas of life:

- **Health:** Sticking to a workout routine or a healthy eating plan requires discipline.
- **School/Work:** Meeting deadlines and completing tasks on time involves ignoring distractions.
- **Money:** Saving, budgeting, and avoiding impulsive purchases need self-control.
- **Relationships:** Being patient, listening well, and handling conflicts calmly can take discipline.

Discipline vs. Motivation

It's easy to confuse discipline with motivation, but they're not the same thing. **Motivation** is the internal drive that makes you excited to do something. It often comes from passion or strong desire. **Discipline**, on the other hand, is about doing the work even when motivation fades. It's the force that says, "I'll do it anyway," because you have made a commitment to yourself.

The Role of Willpower

Willpower is like a mental muscle. You use it whenever you resist temptation or try to focus on a challenging task. Research suggests that willpower can be depleted if you use it too much without rest—similar to how your physical muscles get tired. However, you can train your willpower over time by gradually challenging yourself with tasks that require self-control. For instance, if you find it hard to get up early, you can start by setting your alarm 15 minutes earlier than usual and slowly adjust.

Self-Compassion

While discipline often involves pushing yourself, it's also important to balance it with self-compassion. Self-compassion means treating yourself kindly when you make mistakes or fail to meet your standards. It doesn't mean letting yourself off the hook entirely. Rather, it means acknowledging that everyone struggles sometimes, and encouraging yourself to do better next time. This gentle approach can help you maintain discipline in the long run because it prevents burnout and harsh self-criticism.

Examples of Self-Discipline in Daily Life

- **Turning off phone notifications while studying or working** to stay focused.
- **Going to bed on time** instead of watching one more episode of a TV show.
- **Saving a portion of each paycheck** rather than spending it all.
- **Refusing a second slice of cake** if you're trying to maintain a healthy diet.

Self-discipline is like a guiding force that keeps you aligned with your goals, even when short-term temptations appear. By understanding what it is and why it matters, you set the stage for building it more effectively in your own life.

Section 2: Habit Formation and Routine

One of the most effective ways to strengthen self-discipline is by building good habits and routines. A habit is an action you perform so regularly that it becomes almost automatic—like brushing your teeth or locking your door before leaving home. When something is a habit, you don't have to rely on willpower alone.

How Habits Form

Habits form through repetition. Each time you perform an action under specific conditions, your brain begins to associate the two. For example, if you decide to do a short workout every morning right after waking up, your brain will slowly link "wake up" with "exercise." After enough repetitions, you'll find it feels natural to exercise first thing in the morning.

Creating a Routine

A routine is a set sequence of actions you do every day (or most days) around the same time. Examples:

- Morning routine: Wake up, exercise, shower, eat breakfast, leave for school/work.
- Evening routine: Dinner, tidy up, read a book, plan for the next day, sleep.

Routines reduce the number of decisions you have to make, which saves your willpower. If you know that 7:00 PM is "study time," you don't have to keep deciding whether to study or watch a movie. The choice is already made by your routine.

Starting Small

If you want to build a new habit—like reading for 20 minutes each day—start small. Maybe read for just 5 minutes at first. Once you get comfortable with that, increase the time. This gradual approach is less overwhelming and increases the chance that the habit will stick.

Consistency is Key

It's crucial to practice your new habit or routine consistently. Doing it daily or on a fixed schedule helps your brain recognize it as part of your normal life. If you skip too often, the habit won't form as strongly. That said, missing one day isn't the end of the world. If you slip up, just get back to the habit the next day. The key is consistency over the long haul.

Anchoring New Habits

A helpful trick is to anchor a new habit onto an existing habit. For example, if you already brush your teeth every morning, you can decide that right after brushing your teeth, you'll do 10 push-ups. Attaching the new behavior to an existing one makes it easier to remember and follow through. Over time, both actions can become linked in your mind.

Rewarding Yourself

Positive reinforcement can help solidify habits. For instance, if you complete your daily reading, treat yourself to something small—maybe a healthy snack or a few minutes of your favorite hobby. Celebrating small successes keeps you motivated and trains your brain to look forward to the routine.

Building habits and creating routines might take a bit of effort at first, but once they're in place, they can greatly reduce the mental strain needed to stay disciplined. Essentially, you're putting part of your life on "autopilot" in a beneficial way.

Section 3: Overcoming Procrastination

Procrastination is the act of delaying a task that needs to be done, often in favor of more enjoyable or easier activities. It's a common barrier to self-discipline. You might say, "I'll start tomorrow," or "I'll do this after one more video," and before you know it, hours or even days have passed.

Why We Procrastinate

1. **Fear of Failure:** Sometimes, we avoid tasks because we're afraid we won't do them well.
2. **Lack of Interest:** If the task feels boring, we find it hard to start.
3. **Overwhelm:** If the task seems too big, we don't know where to begin.

4. **Instant Gratification:** We might prefer something fun right now, like chatting with friends or playing games.

Tips to Beat Procrastination

1. **Break Tasks into Smaller Steps:** If you have a big project, identify the first small step you can do right away. For example, if you need to write a paper, start by outlining your main points.
2. **Use Timers or the Pomodoro Technique:** Work for 25 minutes, then take a short 5-minute break. Repeat. These timed intervals help you focus without feeling overwhelmed.
3. **Remove Distractions:** If your phone is a big temptation, put it in another room or turn off notifications while you work.
4. **Set Interim Deadlines:** Instead of having one big deadline, set mini-deadlines along the way.
5. **Reward Progress:** Promise yourself a small reward after completing a chunk of work. This gives you something positive to look forward to.
6. **Know Your "Why":** Constantly remind yourself why the task matters. If you see the task as meaningful, you're more likely to start sooner.

The Role of Self-Talk

Your inner voice can either push you forward or hold you back. If you hear yourself saying, "I'm too tired to start," try countering it with, "I'll just do five minutes." That five-minute promise often makes the task feel more doable, and once you start, you might keep going. Changing your self-talk from "I can't" to "I'll try for a few minutes" can make a big difference.

Getting Help

If procrastination is a major issue, consider getting help from friends, family, or a professional. Having someone check in on your progress can add accountability, which helps you stay on task. Study groups or accountability partners are useful for work or school goals. A mentor or coach might provide structured advice and keep you motivated.

Long-Term View

Understand that overcoming procrastination is a skill you build over time. You might still have days when you struggle. The important thing is to keep practicing the strategies, noticing what works for you, and adjusting as needed. Each time you succeed in starting a task, you reinforce the belief that you can tackle challenges head-on.

Procrastination can rob you of precious time and keep you from achieving your goals. By using techniques like breaking tasks down, setting mini-deadlines, and managing distractions, you can reclaim control of your time and strengthen your self-discipline.

Section 4: Managing Temptations and Urges

Temptations are everywhere. Whether it's junk food when you're trying to eat healthy or entertaining apps when you need to study, urges can distract you from what you truly want. Learning to manage these temptations is a vital part of self-discipline.

Recognizing Your Triggers

A "trigger" is something that sparks a certain behavior or craving. For instance, you might crave sweets whenever you watch TV. Or you might scroll through social media whenever you feel stressed. Identifying these triggers is the first step toward controlling them. Once you're aware of them, you can take steps to avoid or manage them.

Creating Barriers

If you want to resist a temptation, make it harder to access. For instance:

- If you're tempted to play video games instead of studying, store your game console in a closet, out of sight.
- If you tend to snack on junk food, don't buy it in the first place. Or, keep it on a high shelf that requires effort to reach.

- If social media distracts you, delete the apps from your phone or use website blockers during certain hours.

By creating barriers, you force yourself to pause and think before giving in to temptation.

Replacing Negative Habits

Willpower alone might not be enough to resist a strong urge. Instead of just saying "no," try to replace the unwanted behavior with a healthier alternative. If you love snacking while watching TV, replace chips with carrot sticks or fruit. If you always check your phone during study breaks, replace that habit with a quick stretch or a short walk. This "substitution method" ensures you still fulfill your desire for a break or reward, but in a less harmful way.

Practicing Mindfulness

Mindfulness involves being fully present and aware of what you're doing and feeling. When you feel a temptation coming on, pause and notice the thoughts and emotions running through your mind. Ask yourself questions like:

- "Why do I want this right now?"
- "Will this help me reach my goals?"
- "How will I feel afterward?"

Often, simply taking a moment to reflect can lessen the urge. You realize that the temporary pleasure might not be worth the long-term cost.

Delaying Gratification

Another technique is to tell yourself, "I can have this, but not right now." For example, if you really want to watch a movie but have an important assignment due, promise yourself you'll watch the movie after you finish. Delaying gratification trains your brain to handle waiting and can make you more disciplined over time. When you finally get the treat, it also feels more rewarding.

Celebrating Small Victories

Every time you successfully manage a temptation, take a moment to feel good about your choice. This positive reinforcement will make it easier to resist next time. You might not be perfect at this right away, and that's okay. Over time, you'll get better at noticing triggers, creating barriers, and choosing healthier alternatives. Each small victory is a step toward a more disciplined life.

Section 5: Bouncing Back from Setbacks

No matter how disciplined you become, there will be times when you slip. Maybe you waste a whole day watching videos instead of working, or you blow your budget on an impulsive shopping spree. These setbacks can feel discouraging, but they're a normal part of growth.

Acknowledging Mistakes

The first step is to acknowledge you made a mistake. Avoid the urge to make excuses or blame others. Instead, own up to what happened: "I chose to watch videos instead of studying." This honesty sets the stage for learning.

Learning from Failure

Ask yourself: "Why did this happen?" Maybe you didn't schedule your tasks properly or you felt overwhelmed and avoided the work. Understanding the cause helps you prevent a similar slip in the future. For example, if you realize you avoided studying because you felt burned out, you might schedule more frequent breaks next time.

Adjusting Your Plan

If your setback reveals a flaw in your routine or approach, adjust it. Let's say you planned to wake up at 5 AM every day to exercise, but after a week, you found yourself too exhausted to continue. You might adjust your wake-up time to 6 AM or move your exercise to a different part of the day. The key is not to abandon the goal but to adapt the strategy.

Practicing Self-Compassion

It's easy to beat yourself up after failing to maintain discipline. However, negative self-talk like "I'm a failure" or "I'll never succeed" only makes you feel worse, which can lead to giving up. Instead, practice self-compassion. Remind yourself that everyone stumbles and that what matters is trying again. Treat yourself with the same kindness you would offer a friend who made a mistake.

Using Failures as Motivation

Sometimes, a big setback can actually become a strong motivator. When you see how bad it feels to mess up, you might become more determined to avoid that feeling in the future. Maybe you realize that blowing your budget leads to stress, so you become extra careful about spending next month. Turning a negative experience into a lesson is a powerful way to keep growing.

Gradual Progress Over Perfection

Discipline is not about never slipping up. It's about getting back on track quickly and learning from each mistake. You don't need to be perfect; you just need to show steady improvement. Over time, your setbacks will likely become less frequent, and you'll recover from them faster. This shows real growth in self-discipline.

Remember, discipline is like a muscle. Every time you use it, it gets stronger. Every time you slip and then recover, you build resilience. The goal isn't to eliminate failure but to become better at handling it. Each new day is a chance to show yourself that you can stay on track and keep moving toward the life you want.

Section 6: Strengthening Self-Discipline Over Time

Developing self-discipline isn't a one-time event. It's a gradual process that unfolds over weeks, months, or even years. Here are some strategies to keep improving your discipline as you grow and face new challenges.

Regular Self-Assessment

Every now and then, pause and look at how well you're managing your responsibilities and goals. Are you following through on your tasks? Are you procrastinating less than before? Regular self-assessment helps you catch any bad habits that may be creeping in and highlight the good habits that are working well.

Increasing Challenges Slowly

As you get more comfortable with a routine or habit, consider raising the bar slightly. If you've been jogging for 10 minutes a day without fail, move it up to 15 minutes. If you've been studying one hour each evening, try 1.5 hours. Small increases keep you challenged without overwhelming you. This method, often used by athletes and musicians, ensures steady growth in skill and discipline.

Building a Supportive Environment

Self-discipline is easier when your environment supports it. This includes the people around you, the tools and resources you have, and the space you live or work in. Over time, look for ways to make your environment more discipline-friendly. Perhaps that means organizing your workspace, finding a mentor, or joining a community of people with similar goals.

Learning New Techniques

You may discover additional methods to boost your discipline, such as mindfulness practices, time-blocking strategies, or accountability groups.

Keep an open mind and be willing to try new tools. Not every technique will work for you, but experimenting can lead to useful discoveries.

Balancing Rest and Work

Pushing yourself too hard can lead to burnout, which ultimately hurts your discipline. Make sure to schedule breaks, relaxation, and leisure activities. Adequate sleep is especially important because lack of rest can reduce your willpower and make it harder to stay focused. Balance ensures that you have enough energy and motivation to keep up good habits over the long term.

Tracking Improvements

Just like with goals, tracking your discipline can be helpful. You might note how many times you followed your routine this week or how often you resisted a temptation. Looking back on your achievements can motivate you to keep going. It also gives you a record to see how far you've come.

Rewarding Long-Term Effort

While small rewards are great for daily or weekly successes, consider giving yourself a bigger reward for long-term consistency. For instance, if you stick to your exercise routine for three months straight, maybe treat yourself to a new outfit or a special experience. These occasional larger rewards can celebrate your discipline in a meaningful way.

Strengthening self-discipline is like nurturing a plant. It needs consistent care, proper environment, and a bit of patience. Over time, your discipline "muscle" will grow stronger, and tasks that once felt very hard will become easier. This improvement can spill over into all areas of your life, helping you achieve more of your goals and leading to a deeper sense of personal satisfaction.

Section 7: Practical Self-Discipline Exercises

Building discipline can be approached like building any skill—you practice. Below are some exercises that can boost your self-control and willpower:

1. **The "No" Exercise**
   Pick a small temptation you often give in to—such as checking social media frequently. Make a rule that for the next hour (or some set time), you will say "no" each time you feel the urge. This exercise builds your resistance muscle by forcing you to confront urges head-on.
2. **Daily Self-Control Challenge**
   Choose one simple thing each day that requires self-control. For example, if you're craving a sweet snack, delay it by 30 minutes. If you want to buy something impulsively, wait a day before making the purchase. Over time, these small acts strengthen your willpower.
3. **Mindful Eating**
   At least once a day, eat a meal or snack without watching TV or using your phone. Focus on the taste, texture, and smell of your food. Pay attention to your body's signals of hunger and fullness. This mindful approach trains you to be more aware and less impulsive.
4. **Early Wake-Up Practice**
   If waking up is a struggle, aim to get up just 10 minutes earlier than usual. Do this for a week. When that becomes comfortable, move it to 15 or 20 minutes earlier. Each time you follow through, you're proving to yourself you can control your actions rather than letting the alarm clock control you.
5. **Gratitude Pause**
   Set an alarm once a day to pause and reflect on three things you're grateful for. This quick exercise can shift your mindset from "I want what I want now" to "I appreciate what I already have." Gratitude can help reduce cravings and impatience.
6. **Timed Work Sessions**
   Similar to the Pomodoro Technique, commit to a set time (e.g., 25 minutes) to work without distractions, then take a 5-minute break. Repeat this cycle a few times. It helps you practice staying focused on a task, building mental stamina.

7. **Self-Imposed Deadlines**
   Give yourself a personal deadline that's earlier than the official one. If a paper is due in two weeks, pretend it's due in one week. This helps you avoid last-minute cramming and trains you to act with urgency.

These exercises might seem small, but each one is an opportunity to practice controlling your impulses and choosing your long-term goals over short-term desires. Consistency is more important than intensity. Doing these exercises daily or weekly can gradually build a strong foundation of self-discipline.

Section 8: Integrating Discipline with Goal-Setting

Self-discipline and goal-setting are closely linked. Goals outline what you want to achieve, and discipline ensures you do the work needed to reach them.

Matching Discipline to Goals

Review your goals from Chapter 3. Ask yourself, "What daily or weekly habits do I need to maintain to achieve these goals?" This could include study sessions, workout routines, or saving money each month. Discipline helps you stick to these habits even when you're not feeling particularly motivated.

Creating an Action Plan

After identifying the habits you need, form a plan:

1. **Schedule Tasks:** Decide when and where you'll perform each habit.
2. **List Resources:** Write down what you need—books, videos, equipment.
3. **Set Mini-Goals:** If you have a big goal (like writing a book), list smaller targets (one chapter per week) to stay on track.

4. **Decide on Rewards:** Plan small celebrations for each mini-goal reached.

Tracking Both Goals and Discipline

Keep a record not just of your progress toward the end goal, but also of how well you're following your daily discipline habits. For instance, you might mark a calendar each day you complete your planned tasks. If you see a long streak of success, you'll be motivated to keep it going.

Handling Slumps

At some point, you might hit a slump. Maybe your initial excitement fades, or life gets busier. This is a normal part of any long-term process. Revisit your reasons for setting the goal. Remind yourself of how achieving it will improve your life. If needed, tweak your plan to fit your current situation—maybe reduce the frequency of tasks but maintain some level of consistency.

Staying Accountable

Accountability boosts discipline. Share your plan with someone who cares about your success, like a friend, family member, or a study buddy. Check in with them regularly and discuss any struggles. Sometimes, knowing someone else will ask about your progress can be enough to keep you moving forward.

Balancing Ambition and Reality

While it's good to aim high, be realistic about how much self-discipline you can apply at once. Trying to change too many habits overnight can lead to burnout. It's better to succeed at a manageable plan than to fail at an overly ambitious one. Over time, as your discipline grows, you can add more tasks or aim for bigger milestones.

Integrating discipline with goal-setting is like combining a map with the fuel for your car. The map (your goals) shows you where you're going. The fuel (discipline) keeps you moving along the path. Together, they help you reach your destination more smoothly and efficiently.

Section 9: Long-Term Benefits of Self-Discipline

Developing self-discipline has benefits that go far beyond just reaching a single goal. Over time, disciplined behaviors can reshape your entire life.

Enhanced Confidence

Each time you follow through on your promises to yourself, you prove you're capable and reliable. This builds self-trust, which boosts confidence. With increased confidence, you might feel more willing to tackle harder challenges and aim for bigger goals.

Better Relationships

Self-discipline often involves patience, empathy, and active listening. When you learn to control your impulses—like snapping at someone who disagrees with you or interrupting people—you become a better friend, partner, or family member. Over time, this can strengthen your social and emotional connections.

Greater Success in Work or School

Employers, teachers, and colleagues appreciate people who can manage their time and responsibilities well. If you consistently meet deadlines, complete tasks thoroughly, and show up prepared, you're more likely to earn respect and opportunities. Over the years, this can lead to career advancement or academic achievements.

Financial Stability

Discipline with money—like budgeting, saving, and avoiding impulse buys—can lead to better financial health. Over time, you'll accumulate savings, reduce debt, and possibly invest in things that grow your wealth.

This financial security can open up more options in life, such as traveling or starting a small business.

Health and Well-being

Maintaining discipline in areas like exercise, diet, and rest leads to better physical health. This, in turn, boosts mental well-being because a healthy body often supports a healthy mind. You might also feel more energetic and resilient, which helps you handle stress more effectively.

Personal Growth

Discipline encourages you to keep learning, keep trying, and keep improving. Every time you exercise self-control, you strengthen your willpower and problem-solving skills. This constant growth can make you more adaptable in a world that's always changing.

Setting an Example

Whether you realize it or not, people around you—family, friends, even coworkers—notice when you consistently work toward your goals. Your self-discipline can inspire them to be more disciplined in their own lives. You become a role model, showing that steady effort can lead to real results.

Long-Term Happiness

While discipline might sound strict at first, it often leads to deeper satisfaction and happiness. When you achieve goals that align with your values, you feel a sense of purpose. When you're in control of your habits and decisions, you feel empowered. Over time, these positive feelings can become a steady part of your life.

In essence, self-discipline isn't just about short-term wins; it's a lifelong skill that supports almost every area of life. If you keep nurturing it, you may find yourself living a life that feels more stable, more fulfilling, and more in line with who you truly want to be.

Chapter 5: Overcoming Fears and Doubts

Introduction

Fear is a powerful emotion that can stop us from doing things we want or need to do. We can be afraid of failing a test, talking to a new person, or trying a new skill. Sometimes, fear makes us feel shaky, nervous, or even sick to our stomach. Doubt often walks hand in hand with fear. We might think, "What if I'm not good enough? What if people laugh at me?" These worries can grow in our minds until we choose not to act at all.

This chapter will help you learn how to face your fears and deal with doubts. We'll talk about where fear comes from, how it can protect us, and also how it can hold us back. We will look at different types of fears—like fear of failure, fear of rejection, or fear of making mistakes. We'll explore practical steps you can take to handle these feelings and keep moving forward with your goals. By the end of this chapter, you will understand that fear is normal, but it doesn't have to control your life. You can learn to face it bravely and keep growing, even when you feel uncertain or scared.

Section 1: Understanding Fear

Fear is an emotion that signals we sense danger or a threat. In ancient times, fear protected our ancestors from wild animals or dangerous situations. When they felt fear, their bodies would release chemicals that made them run faster or fight harder if they had to defend themselves. This reaction is commonly called "fight or flight." Even now, in modern life, the fight-or-flight response can help us stay alert in emergencies—like if a car swerves suddenly near us, or we face a critical health risk.

However, fear is not always useful in everyday life. Sometimes we feel fear in situations that are not truly dangerous, such as speaking in front of a group or failing a test. Our bodies might still react as if a wild animal were chasing us, which causes shaky hands, a fast heartbeat, or an upset stomach. These physical reactions can make us feel even more anxious or uncertain. At times, this stops us from doing the very things that help us grow—like giving a presentation, trying out for a sports team, or asking for help.

It's important to see that fear itself is not bad. It only becomes a problem when it prevents us from living our lives fully. For example, it's wise to be cautious when crossing a busy road, because the fear of getting hurt makes you look both ways. But letting fear stop you from ever going outside would limit your life in a negative way.

When you understand that fear is a normal response, you start to see it differently. You realize everyone feels afraid sometimes, whether they show it or not. Even the bravest people feel scared—they've just learned to push through it. Understanding that fear can be managed is the first step to overcoming it. Sometimes, simply saying, "I feel scared right now, but that's okay," can help you calm down. Acknowledging your fear, rather than hiding it, gives you power to work with it.

Section 2: Common Types of Fear

There are many types of fear people experience, and each can shape our actions in different ways. Here are some common examples:

1. **Fear of Failure:** Many people worry that they won't succeed at a task, whether it's taking a test, making a speech, or starting a new business. This fear can sometimes stop them from even trying. They might think, "If I never try, I can't fail." But avoiding failure also means missing out on the chance to learn and grow.
2. **Fear of Rejection:** This fear often shows up in social situations. We might be scared that others won't accept us or will judge us harshly. This leads some people to avoid making new friends, sharing ideas, or even talking about their feelings.
3. **Fear of the Unknown:** Many of us like to feel in control. When we face a new or unfamiliar situation—like moving to a different city,

starting a new job, or going to a school we've never been to—we might feel anxious or uneasy because we don't know what will happen.
4. **Fear of Making Mistakes:** Some people want to get everything "perfect" and feel distressed at the thought of an error. This can lead to procrastination or avoiding any challenge where they might fail.
5. **Fear of Change:** Life changes can be unsettling. Whether it's a big change (like a new relationship) or a small one (like a new phone), we might worry about losing what we're used to or not being able to handle the new situation.

Each of these fears might show up in different areas of life. It's important to know that fear doesn't necessarily go away completely. But when you understand the type of fear you're facing, you can use the right strategies to deal with it. For example, if you're afraid of failure, you could work on seeing mistakes as learning opportunities. If you're afraid of rejection, you could practice positive self-talk and remind yourself you're worthy of respect, even if not everyone agrees with you. Understanding the nature of your fear is the first step in finding ways to overcome it.

Section 3: The Role of Doubt

Doubt often appears hand in hand with fear. It's that little voice in your head that whispers, "You can't do this," or "You're not good enough." Doubt can make you question your abilities, even if you have shown skill and determination in other areas. It can also keep you from acting, because you worry about what might happen if you fail or look foolish.

However, doubt is not always negative. Sometimes, a small amount of doubt encourages you to prepare and be cautious. If you doubt your ability to pass a test, you might study harder to prove that doubt wrong. If you doubt your cooking skills, you might practice a recipe a few times before serving it to guests. In this way, doubt can push you to work harder and polish your skills.

But too much doubt can become paralyzing. If you let doubt grow unchecked, it can fill your mind with excuses: "I'm too old to learn this," "I'm just not smart," or "People like me never succeed." When these thoughts dominate, you might not take even the first step toward your goal.

One important thing to remember is that everyone has doubts sometimes, even experts and successful people. They simply learn to keep going despite those doubts. Doubts are thoughts, not facts. You can question them. Instead of assuming that a doubt is true, you can ask, "Do I have evidence for this?" or "Is this really the only possible outcome?" Often, you'll find that doubt is built on fears rather than facts.

A good strategy is to notice when doubt arises, then challenge it. For instance, if you catch yourself thinking, "I'm not good enough," list times you succeeded in a similar situation. Remind yourself of your past achievements or your dedication to learning. Over time, you'll see you have more ability than your doubts want you to believe. By treating doubt as a visitor rather than a permanent resident in your mind, you can keep moving forward, step by step.

Section 4: Identifying the Source of Your Fear

Before you can face your fear, it helps to figure out where it comes from. Sometimes, the cause of fear is obvious: you touched a hot stove once and burned your hand, so now you're extra careful around stoves. Other times, fear has roots in our past experiences or beliefs. Maybe you grew up with people who criticized you often, making you afraid to try new things. Or perhaps you had a bad experience giving a presentation, so now you freeze up whenever you speak in front of others.

Ask yourself questions to pinpoint the source of your fear:

- **When did I first feel this fear?**
- **What happened that made me think I should be afraid?**

- **Is there a particular event or memory that triggers this fear?**

Sometimes, the answer might surprise you. You might discover that your fear of swimming, for example, started because you once slipped near a pool when you were little. Or you might realize you fear rejection because you were teased in school. Knowing the source doesn't magically make the fear disappear, but it can help you see it in a different light.

Also, consider if your current environment or relationships are feeding your fears. If you have friends who constantly discourage you, you might feel more fearful about your abilities. If you watch scary news stories all day, you might begin to fear the world is a dangerous place. Part of overcoming fear is choosing what you expose yourself to and who you spend time with.

Finally, ask yourself if your fear is realistic. For instance, if you're afraid of flying, look at the actual statistics on airplane safety. Often, we find that our fears are larger in our minds than they are in real life. By identifying the root cause and examining the evidence, we can start to reduce the intensity of our fear, one step at a time.

Section 5: Techniques to Overcome Fear

Overcoming fear isn't about never feeling scared again. It's about moving forward even when fear is present. Here are some practical techniques:

1. **Breathing Exercises:** When you feel fear rising, your heart might race and your breathing might become quick. Try slowing your breath. Inhale deeply through your nose for four seconds, hold for a second, then exhale slowly through your mouth for four seconds. Repeat several times. This helps calm the physical reaction to fear, sending signals to your brain that you are safe.
2. **Gradual Exposure:** If a certain situation scares you—like talking to new people—try exposing yourself to it in small steps. You might start by speaking up in front of one friend, then a small group, then a larger audience. Each small success builds your confidence and shows you that you can handle it.

3. **Positive Visualization:** Close your eyes and imagine yourself succeeding in the situation you fear. If you're afraid of a big exam, picture yourself calmly answering questions, feeling prepared, and finishing on time. Visualization can train your brain to expect a positive outcome, which can reduce anxiety.
4. **Self-Talk and Affirmations:** Replace negative thoughts like, "I'm going to fail," with supportive statements like, "I'm prepared, and I can do this." Simple affirmations such as "I am brave" or "I can handle challenges" might feel odd at first, but repeating them can shift your mindset over time.
5. **Seek Knowledge or Training:** Sometimes, fear comes from not knowing what to expect. If you fear public speaking, take a class or watch videos on how to present effectively. Gaining skills and knowledge reduces the unknown and boosts your confidence.
6. **Talk to Someone:** Sharing your fears with a friend, family member, or counselor can help you see the situation more clearly. They might offer advice or simply listen, which can lighten the emotional load. Talking about your fear can also help you realize that you're not alone—many people feel the same way.
7. **Set Small Goals:** If your fear is tied to a big dream—like starting a business—break it into smaller tasks. Focus on one task at a time instead of the entire project. Each step you complete successfully weakens your fear, showing you that progress is possible.

All these techniques work best when you practice them regularly. It might take some time to see big changes, but each small step forward is a victory. Overcoming fear is a skill you build with patience and consistent effort, much like learning a new sport or instrument.

Section 6: Building Self-Confidence

Self-confidence is the belief that you can handle the challenges life throws your way. It doesn't mean you think you're perfect or better than others. It just means you trust your ability to learn, adapt, and keep trying. Building self-confidence can lower fear and doubt because you're more willing to take risks and recover from mistakes.

Ways to Boost Confidence:

1. **Acknowledge Past Successes:** Make a list of times you achieved something you once thought was hard. This can be anything—learning to ride a bike, passing a tough exam, or resolving a conflict with a friend. Reminding yourself of these successes shows you that you have the ability to overcome obstacles.
2. **Practice:** Skills improve with practice, whether it's playing an instrument or speaking another language. The more you practice, the more you see your progress, and this naturally boosts your confidence.
3. **Set Achievable Goals:** If you're always aiming for goals far beyond your current level, you might feel like you're failing too often. Instead, set goals that stretch you a little but are still reachable. Each time you succeed, you'll feel more confident about moving to the next level.
4. **Positive Environment:** Spend time with people who cheer you on. A supportive environment can make a huge difference in how you see yourself. Avoid those who constantly put you down or make you question your worth.
5. **Body Language:** Sometimes, confidence starts with simple physical actions. Stand up straight, keep your head up, and make eye contact when you talk. These small changes can send messages to your brain that you're capable and strong.
6. **Avoid Perfectionism:** Trying to be perfect all the time can hurt your confidence because no one can achieve perfection. Learn to aim for "good enough" and be proud of steady progress rather than flawless results.

By actively working on your self-confidence, you give yourself a sturdy foundation for dealing with fear and doubt. You start to trust that even if things go wrong, you can handle the fallout and learn from it. Over time, this trust in your own abilities helps you face challenges with more courage and less worry.

Section 7: Embracing Failure as a Learning Tool

Most people want to avoid failure because it's uncomfortable and often embarrassing. However, failure can be one of the greatest teachers in life. When you fail at something, you get specific feedback on what didn't work. You learn what you can improve or change next time.

Why Failure Matters:

1. **Experience:** Each failure is an experience that adds to your understanding of yourself and the situation. Maybe you learn that you need better time management or a different approach to studying.
2. **Resilience:** Failing and then picking yourself back up develops mental strength. It proves that you can survive mistakes and still move forward.
3. **Innovation:** Many great inventions and breakthroughs happened after multiple failures. People tried different methods, learned from each flop, and eventually found a formula that worked.

Changing Your View of Failure:

- **From "I Failed" to "I Learned":** Instead of saying "I failed my math test," say "I learned I need more practice on fractions." This simple change in language helps you focus on growth rather than defeat.
- **Focus on the Process:** Notice the steps you took, what went right, and what went wrong. If you see mistakes as part of the process, they don't feel so frightening.
- **Celebrate Small Wins:** Even if the overall result wasn't what you wanted, identify parts of the process you did well. Recognizing these smaller successes can give you the energy to try again.

Taking Action After Failure:

After a failed attempt, take a moment to reflect. What did you learn? What would you do differently next time? Use this insight to make a clear plan.

Then, jump back into action with the new knowledge you gained. By treating failure as an event rather than an identity, you keep your sense of self-worth intact. You are not a failure; you are a person who experienced a setback.

Embracing failure doesn't mean you aim to fail on purpose. It means you understand it's a natural part of trying new things. When you realize that failure is not the end but a stepping stone, fear loses some of its power. You become more willing to take risks because you know a mistake isn't permanent defeat. It's just another lesson on the road to success.

Section 8: Handling Doubt from Others

Sometimes, the doubts we face don't come from ourselves. They come from people around us—family, friends, or even strangers who say, "You can't do that," or "That's too hard for someone like you." Hearing these doubts can be painful, especially if you respect the person who's doubting you.

Why People Cast Doubt:

1. **Their Own Fears:** They might be afraid of failure themselves and project that onto you.
2. **Lack of Understanding:** If they don't understand your goals or dreams, they might think those goals are impossible.
3. **Protectiveness:** Sometimes, loved ones doubt your plans because they worry you'll get hurt. They want to keep you safe, even if that means discouraging you.

How to Respond:

- **Listen, But Filter:** Sometimes, people have useful feedback even if they express it as doubt. For instance, if someone says you're not ready to run a marathon next week, maybe they're pointing out you need more training. Filter out the harsh tone but keep any useful information.

- **Stay True to Your Vision:** If you truly believe in your goal, keep working toward it. You can acknowledge other people's concerns but still decide for yourself.
- **Show Them Your Progress:** Sometimes, seeing you make small steps forward can change a doubter's mind. If they realize you're serious and capable, they might become supportive over time.
- **Seek Support Elsewhere:** If certain people always doubt you and never provide helpful advice, it might be best to distance yourself from their negativity. Instead, look for mentors, friends, or groups who believe in growth.

Guarding Your Self-Esteem:

Try not to let others' doubts define you. Remind yourself why you started this journey in the first place. Keep your self-talk positive and focus on evidence of your abilities. Maybe you keep a journal where you list your achievements daily, no matter how small. This helps you maintain a sense of confidence and control.

In the end, other people's doubt can only hurt you if you let it. While it's important to consider feedback carefully, you are the one living your life. By staying committed to your path and surrounding yourself with supportive people, you can rise above the doubts others put on you.

Section 9: Real-Life Examples of Overcoming Fear

Sometimes, a story can inspire us more than just words of advice. Here are a few simple examples of how different people overcame their fears:

1. **Facing the Fear of Public Speaking:**
   Priya always dreaded speaking in front of others. Her heart would pound, and her mouth would go dry whenever she had to present. To overcome this, she joined a public speaking club that met once a week. At first, she only gave very short talks. Gradually, she became more comfortable. After a few months, she volunteered to speak for

her class. Although she still felt nervous, she managed to finish her presentation successfully. That small win boosted her confidence, and now she no longer avoids speaking events.

2. **Overcoming Fear of Failure in Sports:**
Gabriel loved basketball but rarely tried out for school teams because he feared failing. He was worried he wouldn't make the cut. After a talk with his coach, he decided to change his mindset. He practiced daily, focused on improving his dribbling and shooting, and reminded himself that failing once wouldn't define him. The first tryout he attended, he didn't make the team. However, instead of giving up, he kept practicing. The next year, he tried again and earned a spot on the roster. Looking back, he realized the fear of failure was bigger in his mind than in reality.

3. **Conquering Fear of Rejection in Friendships:**
Hina often felt lonely but was too scared to reach out to new people. She feared they wouldn't like her. One day, she decided to invite a classmate to study together. Even though she felt anxious, she went ahead and asked. The classmate said yes, and they became good study partners and eventually friends. Encouraged by this success, Hina started joining more group activities. She discovered that while not everyone would become her best friend, most people were open to chatting and getting to know her.

4. **Tackling Fear of the Unknown by Starting a Small Business:**
James had a hobby making handmade soaps. His friends said he should sell them, but he was afraid he didn't know enough about business. After months of doubt, he did research online, watched tutorials, and talked to a local shop owner for tips. Slowly, he started selling his soaps at small craft fairs. Each sale gave him more courage. Today, he runs a small online store. He admits the unknown was scary at first, but learning step by step reduced his fear.

These examples show that everyone has fears, but with patience, practice, and a willingness to take small steps, those fears can be overcome. It's rarely about huge leaps. Instead, it's about steady progress and learning from each experience.

Chapter 6: Developing Healthy Habits

Introduction

Habits are the small actions we do every day, often without even thinking. Some habits make our lives better, like brushing our teeth or washing our hands. Others can hold us back, like overeating junk food or spending too much time on our phones. The good news is that habits can be changed or replaced. By choosing healthy habits, we set ourselves up for better physical health, stronger mental well-being, and more energy to chase our goals.

In this chapter, we'll look at different kinds of healthy habits you can develop—ranging from physical activities and good nutrition to mental exercises and healthy social interactions. We'll talk about practical ways to build these habits into your daily life so they become as natural as brushing your teeth. We'll also discuss the concept of habit stacking (pairing a new habit with one you already have) and ways to track your progress without feeling overwhelmed. By the end of this chapter, you'll have a clear picture of how to create and maintain healthy habits that support your overall personal growth. Healthy habits don't require superhuman willpower; they just need small, consistent steps in the right direction.

Section 1: What Are Healthy Habits?

Healthy habits are actions that improve your physical, mental, or emotional well-being. These actions can vary for each person, but generally, they promote good health, manage stress, and help you build a balanced life. Examples include:

1. **Regular Exercise:** Walking, running, dancing, or any movement that gets your heart rate up and your muscles working.

2. **Balanced Diet:** Eating a variety of nutrient-rich foods, such as fruits, vegetables, whole grains, and lean proteins, while limiting sugary and fatty foods.
3. **Proper Sleep:** Getting enough rest (usually 7–9 hours for adults, more for teenagers and children) to let your body and mind recharge.
4. **Mindfulness Practices:** Activities like meditation or simple breathing exercises that help you stay present and reduce stress.
5. **Social Connections:** Maintaining friendships, family bonds, or joining community groups. Human connection supports emotional health.
6. **Personal Hobbies:** Engaging in enjoyable activities like reading, painting, or playing music to keep your mind creative and relaxed.

Healthy habits don't have to be complicated or expensive. Small steps can have a big impact over time. For instance, a short walk after dinner can boost your mood and help with digestion. Drinking water instead of soda can help you stay hydrated and lower sugar intake. Practicing a short mindfulness exercise before bed can help you sleep better.

Many people think that you need to overhaul your entire lifestyle to be healthy, but that's not true. Often, making one small change and sticking to it can lead to other positive changes. When you start feeling better from one healthy habit, you might be more motivated to add another. Over time, these habits can form a strong foundation that supports your goals and helps you handle stress more easily. The key is consistency—doing healthy actions regularly until they become second nature.

Section 2: Physical Health Habits

Exercise

One of the best habits for physical health is regular exercise. You don't need a fancy gym membership or special equipment. Start by finding an activity you enjoy. It could be playing basketball with friends, dancing in your living room, or going for walks in your neighborhood. Aim for at least

30 minutes of moderate activity most days of the week. If that sounds like too much, begin with 10 or 15 minutes and work your way up. Consistency is what matters most.

Balanced Eating

Eating a balanced diet means getting a variety of nutrients. One simple rule is to include more whole foods—like fruits, vegetables, whole grains, and lean meats—while cutting back on processed snacks and sugary beverages. It also helps to pay attention to portion sizes. Eating until you're 80% full, rather than stuffed, can prevent overeating. If cooking every day seems overwhelming, try meal prepping once or twice a week. You can make a big batch of healthy food and store it for quick meals.

Hydration

Water is essential for almost every function in the body. Keep a water bottle nearby during the day. If you find plain water boring, add slices of fruit like lemon or cucumber for flavor. Staying hydrated can improve your energy levels, help with digestion, and even keep your skin clearer.

Good Posture

Many of us spend hours sitting, whether at school, work, or in front of a screen. Over time, poor posture can cause back pain and stiffness. Make it a habit to sit up straight, keep your shoulders relaxed, and place your feet flat on the floor. Take breaks to stand and stretch every hour. These small habits can make a big difference in preventing aches and pains.

Regular Check-ups

Part of caring for your physical health is visiting healthcare professionals regularly. This includes annual check-ups with a doctor, dental cleanings, and eye exams if needed. Catching potential health issues early can save you from bigger problems down the road. Think of it as regular maintenance, just like taking your car in for a tune-up.

Putting these physical health habits into place isn't always easy, especially if you're juggling a busy schedule. But even small changes—like a 10-minute walk or swapping sugary drinks for water—can add up. Over time, these habits can boost your energy, mood, and overall well-being, making it easier for you to tackle other goals in life.

Section 3: Mental and Emotional Health Habits

Your mental and emotional well-being is just as important as your physical health. Healthy habits in this area help you handle stress, build resilience, and feel more content day to day.

Mindfulness and Meditation

Mindfulness is the practice of paying attention to the present moment without judgment. It can be as simple as taking a few deep breaths and noticing how your body feels. Meditation goes a step further by setting aside dedicated time—maybe 5 or 10 minutes each day—to sit quietly and focus on your breathing or a calming image. Studies suggest that regular meditation can reduce stress and anxiety.

Journaling

Writing down your thoughts and feelings can be a healthy outlet for emotions. You can keep a simple diary or try specific journaling prompts—like listing three things you're grateful for each day. Journaling helps you process experiences, track your mood, and even brainstorm solutions to problems. Over time, it can offer insights into patterns in your thoughts and feelings.

Limiting Negative Input

It's easy to get caught up in negative news stories or social media drama. While staying informed is important, constantly consuming bad news or negative comments can take a toll on your mental health. Try setting a limit—like 15 minutes of news or social media a day—and then focus on more uplifting or educational content.

Talking to Someone

Sometimes, the simplest way to manage stress or sadness is to share your feelings with a trustworthy friend or family member. If issues feel too big or overwhelming, consider talking to a mental health professional like a counselor or therapist. There's no shame in seeking help—just as you'd see a doctor for a physical ailment, you can see a professional for emotional or mental struggles.

Practicing Gratitude

Taking a moment each day to think about what you're thankful for can shift your mindset from negative to positive. It could be something small, like enjoying a good meal, or something big, like having supportive friends. By focusing on gratitude, you train your brain to look for the good in your life, which can boost your overall happiness.

Developing these mental and emotional health habits can make you more resilient when facing life's ups and downs. They help you cope with stress, prevent burnout, and maintain a sense of balance in your daily life.

Section 4: Building Social and Relationship Habits

Humans are social creatures. Our relationships—whether with friends, family, coworkers, or community members—play a big role in our well-being. Developing healthy social habits can improve your emotional health, provide support during tough times, and create a sense of belonging.

Active Listening

One simple habit is to truly listen when someone talks to you. Instead of thinking about what you'll say next, focus on what they're saying. Ask follow-up questions and try to understand their viewpoint. This habit strengthens bonds and shows respect.

Consistent Communication

Regularly check in with people who matter to you. A quick text, call, or short visit can go a long way in maintaining close connections. It's easy to get busy and let weeks or months pass without talking to friends or family. Scheduling a regular catch-up time can keep relationships strong.

Sharing Positive News

Make it a habit to share good news or uplifting stories with the people you care about. Celebrating each other's wins, no matter how small, can build a positive atmosphere. This might involve congratulating a friend on a job milestone or simply sharing funny moments from your day.

Setting Boundaries

Healthy relationships also mean respecting each other's boundaries. If you need time alone to recharge, communicate that in a kind way. Likewise, if a friend is draining your energy by constantly complaining or criticizing, it's okay to set limits on how often or how long you interact. Good boundaries protect your emotional health and prevent resentments from building up.

Acts of Kindness

Small acts of kindness—like offering help, giving compliments, or doing volunteer work—can enrich your social habits. Not only do these actions help others, but they also boost your own sense of well-being. Research shows that giving to others can make you feel happier, more connected, and even less stressed.

By developing these social habits, you create a network of support that can buffer life's challenges. Whether it's active listening, staying in touch, or setting boundaries, these practices help ensure your relationships remain healthy and supportive over time.

Section 5: Habit Stacking and Routine-Building

Forming a new habit often feels easier when you attach it to an existing routine. This method is called "habit stacking." The idea is to take a habit you already do regularly—like brushing your teeth—and add a new action right before or after it. For example, if you want to start meditating, you could stack that habit onto your morning teeth-brushing. Right after you finish brushing, you spend five minutes meditating. Over time, your brain starts to link those two actions, making it feel natural to meditate after brushing your teeth.

Steps for Habit Stacking:

1. **Pick a Current Routine:** Identify something you do every day without fail—this might be making coffee, taking a shower, or feeding a pet.
2. **Add One Small Action:** Choose one simple, new habit you want to form. It should be small enough that it's not overwhelming. If you want to drink more water, place a glass of water next to your coffee maker and drink it right after you start the coffee.
3. **Keep It Consistent:** Do the new action every time you follow your old routine. Consistency teaches your brain to see these actions as connected.
4. **Reward Yourself:** Give yourself a mental pat on the back or a small treat whenever you complete the new habit. Over time, the good feeling will reinforce the behavior.

Building a Daily Routine

A routine is a set schedule of habits that you perform in a specific order. For instance, a morning routine might look like: wake up, drink water, stretch, shower, eat breakfast, then start work or school. A nighttime routine might include: a quick tidy-up of your room, preparing clothes for the next day, reading a book, and then going to sleep.

Benefits of Routines:

- **Reduced Decision Fatigue:** You don't spend energy figuring out what to do next.
- **Improved Efficiency:** You get more done in less time because you're following a set sequence.
- **Lower Stress:** Having predictable habits can make your day feel more stable.

Remember that your routine should fit your life and priorities. If you hate running in the morning, don't force yourself into a morning run routine. Maybe you can walk in the afternoon or do a brief yoga session before bed. The key is finding routines that feel sustainable and serve your goals, rather than copying someone else's schedule.

With habit stacking and well-crafted routines, you can build healthy actions into your day without feeling overwhelmed. Over time, these small changes lead to big results.

Section 6: Tracking and Celebrating Progress

Once you start working on healthy habits, it helps to keep track of what you're doing. This can be as simple as marking an "X" on a calendar each day you complete your habit. You can also use a notebook, spreadsheet, or phone app to log your actions.

Why Track Your Habits?

1. **Measurable Progress:** Seeing a chain of days where you followed through on your habit can motivate you to keep going.
2. **Identifying Patterns:** If you notice you always skip your workout on Fridays, you can plan around that—maybe by scheduling a rest day on Fridays or changing your workout time.
3. **Accountability:** If you share your progress with a friend or a group, you feel responsible for sticking with your plan.

Types of Tracking:

- **Paper Calendar or Planner:** A simple check mark each day you do your habit.
- **Habit Tracker Journal:** A grid where you fill in boxes for each habit.
- **Digital Apps:** Many apps send reminders and show you colorful charts of your progress.

Celebrating Small Wins

When you hit milestones—like a week or a month of consistent habits—take time to celebrate. The celebration doesn't have to be fancy or expensive. It could be treating yourself to a favorite snack, buying a new book, or simply recognizing your achievement with a relaxing activity. This positive reinforcement makes you more likely to stick with your new habits.

Be sure to keep your celebrations balanced with your goals. For instance, if your habit is about eating healthier, maybe don't celebrate by bingeing on junk food. Instead, pick a reward that aligns with your broader goals—like a fresh fruit smoothie or a new workout accessory.

In the long run, tracking and celebrating might seem like small steps, but they can keep you motivated and aware of your progress. You see that your efforts are paying off, which encourages you to maintain or even expand your healthy habits.

Section 7: Overcoming Obstacles and Staying Consistent

Even the best habits can be challenged by life's twists and turns. Here's how to overcome common obstacles and remain consistent:

1. **Time Constraints:** Busy schedules make it tough to maintain new habits. One solution is to start very small. If you're too busy for a 30-minute workout, do a 5-minute workout or a quick stretch. It's better to do a little than nothing at all.
2. **Loss of Motivation:** There will be days when you just don't feel like sticking to your habit. This is where discipline (from Chapter 4) comes in. Remind yourself why you started. Focus on the benefits you've seen, even if they're small.
3. **Stress and Emotional Upsets:** When we're stressed, we might turn to old, unhealthy habits like comfort eating or skipping exercise. Try to have a plan in place for stress—a calming playlist, a short walk, or calling a supportive friend. Having a healthy coping strategy can keep you from defaulting to negative habits.
4. **Travel or Unusual Schedules:** Vacations or travel can disrupt routines. Plan ahead by adapting your habit to the new environment. For instance, if you're traveling, pack healthy snacks or look for local walking paths to get some exercise.
5. **Plateaus:** Sometimes, you might stop seeing progress. For example, you might lose some weight or gain strength at first, then it levels off. This is normal. Adjust your routine—try a new exercise, change your meal plan slightly, or add more variety to your hobbies—to keep improving.
6. **Negative Influences:** If people around you have unhealthy habits, it can be harder to stay on track. Let them know you're trying to make positive changes. If they don't support you, do your best to stick to your plan anyway, or find a new group (online or in person) that shares your health goals.

Overcoming these obstacles requires creativity, patience, and a willingness to adapt. The key is not to expect perfection. You will have slip-ups or missed days. The important thing is to restart as soon as possible, learning from the challenges and using them to grow stronger in your commitment to healthy living.

Section 8: Making Healthy Habits a Lifelong Practice

Building healthy habits is not a one-time project—it's a lifelong journey. As you grow and your life changes, your habits might need to adapt. For example, the exercise routine you had as a teenager might be different from what you need in your 30s or 40s. The key is to remain flexible and keep learning.

Long-Term Mindset

Instead of focusing on quick fixes (like crash diets or sudden intense workout plans), think about what you can maintain for years. Sustainable changes are more valuable than big short-term gains. A short diet might help you lose a few pounds, but if you return to old eating habits right after, you'll gain the weight back. Instead, find a balanced eating pattern you enjoy and can stick with.

Periodic Check-Ins

Schedule regular times—maybe once every three months—to review your habits. Ask yourself:

- **Are these habits still helping me?**
- **Do I need to adjust anything?**
- **Have my goals or interests changed?**

This check-in helps you catch any drifting away from good practices and lets you modify habits to fit your current situation.

Variety and Fun

If you get bored with the same workout routine or the same lunch every day, look for ways to add variety. Try new recipes, explore different exercise options, or pick up a new hobby. Keeping things fresh prevents monotony and keeps you engaged in your healthy lifestyle.

Celebrating Growth

Over the years, you might see major improvements in your health, mood, and overall well-being. Pause to acknowledge these changes. You might notice you're more confident in social situations or have more energy to play with your kids. These positive outcomes are worth celebrating, and they remind you why these habits are so valuable.

By treating healthy habits as a flexible, long-term part of your life, you give yourself the best chance at ongoing growth. It's not about being perfect. It's about making steady, positive choices that support your health and happiness for many years to come.

Chapter 7: Growing Through Challenges and Failure

Introduction

Life is full of ups and downs. Sometimes things go well, and we feel confident. Other times, we face problems or even fail at what we try to do. These moments can be painful, but they can also help us grow. When we learn from our failures and keep trying, we become stronger and wiser.

In this chapter, we will look at how challenges and failures can help us become better. We'll talk about why failure is not the end of the road, but instead a sign that we are trying new things and learning new lessons. We'll also explore how to face big or small challenges with a positive mindset, even when we feel discouraged. If you've ever felt like giving up after a setback, this chapter can offer you hope and guidance.

No one likes to fail or face difficulties, but these events are often the key to real growth. By the end of this chapter, you'll see that every challenge—whether it's a bad grade on a test, a conflict at work, or a health problem—can offer valuable lessons. With the right perspective, you can use these experiences to become stronger, more empathetic, and better prepared for future obstacles. Let's dive in and learn how to turn challenges and failures into stepping stones toward personal development.

Section 1: Why We Need Challenges

Challenges can be frustrating and even scary. However, they serve an important purpose in our lives:

1. **They Build Resilience:** When we face a tough situation, we have to stretch ourselves to solve it. This "stretching" process builds resilience, which is our ability to bounce back from difficulties. A

person who has never faced any challenge might have a harder time dealing with big problems later on.
2. **They Spark Growth:** Imagine never having a difficult test in school. You might never study deeply, so you'd learn less. When a challenge forces you to work harder, you learn more. This can be true for academic challenges, social challenges (like resolving conflicts), or physical challenges (like training for a sport).
3. **They Reveal Hidden Strengths:** Sometimes, we don't realize what we're capable of until we're pushed. A person who doubts their ability to speak in public might find a hidden talent for storytelling once they actually try. Challenges can uncover skills or qualities we didn't know we had.
4. **They Teach Problem-Solving Skills:** Dealing with a challenge often means breaking it down into smaller parts, looking for possible solutions, and testing them. Each time you solve a problem, you learn a method or principle that could help you solve future problems. This is how great inventors and scientists work—they face challenges, try solutions, fail, learn, and try again.
5. **They Build Confidence:** Successfully handling a challenge, no matter how small, can boost your confidence. If you manage to learn a new skill even though it was hard at first, you'll feel proud. This confidence makes it easier to face the next challenge with a can-do attitude.

Without challenges, life might feel safe, but we wouldn't grow much. We might stay in our comfort zones, never testing the boundaries of our abilities. Challenges, while uncomfortable, push us forward. They make us question old habits, learn new strategies, and become better people overall.

It's important to note that not all challenges are created equal. Some might be big—like dealing with an illness or losing a job—while others might be small—like fixing a minor mistake on a work project. But in every case, challenges have something to teach us. When we approach them with curiosity and determination, we can turn even the hardest moments into opportunities for growth.

Section 2: Understanding Failure

Failure is something many of us fear. We don't like feeling embarrassed, let down, or judged by others. Yet failure is a natural part of the learning process. It signals that we attempted something that didn't work out as planned. Here are a few things to remember about failure:

1. **Failure Is Not the End:** One failure doesn't mean you're doomed to fail at everything. It just means a specific approach didn't work. Many famous people experienced repeated failures before they found success. Their big breakthroughs often came because they kept learning from each attempt.
2. **Failure Teaches Us What Doesn't Work:** When Thomas Edison was inventing the lightbulb, he tried many materials for the filament and failed hundreds of times. Each failure taught him which materials didn't work, which led him closer to the material that did. In our own lives, a failed relationship can teach us about what we need in a partner, or a failed test can show us our weak points in a subject.
3. **Failure Builds Perseverance:** People who never fail might not have developed the perseverance to keep going when things get tough. Failing and bouncing back is how we build our "mental muscle." Over time, we learn to keep trying in the face of setbacks.
4. **Failure Can Be Redefined:** Instead of seeing failure as a dead-end, see it as feedback. It's information that something in your plan or actions needs adjusting. By adjusting, you grow. This perspective shift makes failure less scary and more useful. Think of it as part of the path, not a roadblock.
5. **Failure Encourages Innovation:** Sometimes we only think creatively when we have to fix a failure. If everything is running smoothly, we may have no reason to innovate or improve. Failure pushes us to think outside the box, and that can lead to breakthroughs we wouldn't have considered otherwise.

It's also important to handle failure with self-compassion. Beating yourself up or calling yourself names after you fail only makes it harder to bounce back. Recognize that mistakes are part of being human. Treat yourself with the same kindness you would show a friend who is struggling. Remember, failure is a sign that you were brave enough to try, and trying is how we move forward in life.

Section 3: Common Reactions to Challenges and Failure

When we face challenges or fail at something, we all react differently. Some reactions are more helpful than others. Here are a few common responses and why they matter:

1. **Avoidance:** A person who fears failure might refuse to try in the first place. They might say, "I won't enter the art contest because I'll lose anyway." Avoidance can protect us from immediate disappointment, but it also blocks growth and the chance to learn new things. Over time, people who consistently avoid challenges may feel stuck or regretful.
2. **Blame:** Sometimes, after failing, we look for someone else to blame. It could be blaming a teacher, a coworker, or even "bad luck." While external factors can play a role, blaming others too quickly prevents us from examining our own mistakes or weaknesses. Without honest reflection, we can't improve.
3. **Self-Criticism:** It's natural to feel bad after failing, but some people turn to harsh self-criticism: "I'm so stupid," "I can't do anything right," or "I'm a total loser." This negative inner voice can damage self-esteem and create fear of trying again. It's important to challenge these thoughts by focusing on what you can learn rather than labeling yourself negatively.
4. **Denial:** Denial is when we pretend the failure or challenge isn't a big deal or isn't real. For example, you might keep telling yourself, "I didn't really want that goal anyway," or "It's not my fault at all." While it can help reduce shame temporarily, denial often leads to unresolved problems and repeated mistakes.
5. **Acceptance and Learning:** This is the ideal reaction. We acknowledge the failure or challenge, recognize our emotions, and then think about what lessons can be drawn. We ask, "What could I do differently next time? How did this experience help me grow?" Acceptance doesn't mean you enjoy failing; it just means you understand it's part of the process.

6. **Seeking Help:** Another healthy response is to reach out for support. Talk to a mentor, a friend, or a family member about the challenge or failure. Sometimes, an outside perspective can help you see the situation more clearly. This approach can also remind you that you're not alone—everyone struggles sometimes.

Our reactions matter because they shape what we do next. If we react with avoidance, blame, self-criticism, or denial, we shut down opportunities for growth. But if we accept the challenge or failure, learn from it, and possibly seek help, we can bounce back stronger than before.

Section 4: Practical Steps to Bounce Back

Facing a challenge or failing at something can feel overwhelming at first. Here are some practical steps you can take to bounce back and keep moving:

1. **Pause and Breathe:** When you realize something has gone wrong—like you've failed a test or a project didn't work out—take a moment to pause. Try a few deep breaths to calm your body. This helps you avoid panicking or making rash decisions based on emotion alone.
2. **Acknowledge Your Feelings:** It's normal to feel disappointed, upset, or even angry. Naming your feelings—like saying to yourself, "I feel really sad right now"—can help you process them more easily. Bottling up emotions can lead to stress later on.
3. **Ask Questions:** Once you're calmer, explore what went wrong. Some helpful questions include:
    - "What was my goal?"
    - "What did I do to try to reach it?"
    - "What part of my plan worked, and what part didn't?"
    - "Was I missing any information or resources?"
    - "Could I have asked for help earlier?"
4. Answering these questions honestly can offer clues about how to improve.

5. **Learn and Adjust:** Based on your answers, decide how you will adjust your strategy for next time. Maybe you need more practice, better time management, or a different approach entirely. If you failed a test because you studied only the night before, plan a study schedule for the next time. If your small business idea failed, list the mistakes you made and how you'll avoid them in the future.
6. **Take Small Steps Forward:** Once you have a new plan, break it into small, actionable steps. This makes the next attempt less intimidating. For example, if you need to improve your public speaking skills, start by practicing short talks to a friend, then gradually move to bigger audiences.
7. **Seek Support or Feedback:** Don't hesitate to ask for help from someone more experienced. You might share your new plan with a friend or mentor and ask for their thoughts. Getting feedback can help you spot blind spots you might not see on your own.
8. **Celebrate Improvement:** Even if you haven't reached your ultimate goal yet, celebrate the steps you're taking to bounce back. If you improve your test score next time, even if it's still not perfect, acknowledge that progress. Each small win builds momentum and helps you keep going.

By following these steps, you transform a setback into a chance to learn and grow. You're training your mind to see challenges and failures as temporary obstacles rather than permanent dead-ends.

Section 5: Mindset Shifts for Growth

Overcoming challenges and learning from failure often requires a shift in mindset. Here are some beliefs that can support this positive change:

1. **"Mistakes Are Lessons, Not Punishments."**
   If you see each mistake as a lesson, you'll be less afraid to try new things. You won't feel as though you're being punished by making an error. Instead, you'll think, "Okay, I learned something new about what doesn't work."

2. **"I Haven't Succeeded Yet."**
   Adding the word "yet" to statements like "I can't do this" can change your perspective. Instead of thinking, "I can't do math," say, "I can't do math yet." This small word implies that you're still learning and that success is possible with time and effort.
3. **"Feedback Helps Me Grow."**
   Sometimes, we take feedback as criticism. But feedback—whether from teachers, peers, or coworkers—can point out areas for improvement. If you teach yourself to value feedback, you can make changes faster.
4. **"I Can Learn to Be More Resilient."**
   Resilience isn't something you either have or don't have. You can build it by facing small challenges, learning from them, and moving on to bigger challenges. Over time, you realize you can handle more than you once thought.
5. **"Progress Over Perfection."**
   Aiming for perfection can cause stress and fear of failure. If you focus on making steady progress, you give yourself permission to be a work in progress. Each step forward is a victory.
6. **"Growth Takes Time."**
   Whether it's mastering a musical instrument or learning a new language, progress doesn't happen overnight. Accepting that real growth takes time helps you stay patient when results don't appear right away.

Putting These Beliefs into Practice

- **Use Affirmations:** Repeat positive statements, such as "I am learning every day," or "I can find solutions to problems," especially when you feel discouraged.
- **Surround Yourself with Growth-Minded People:** People who share these beliefs can reinforce them. If your friends believe in learning from failure, you'll feel more comfortable taking risks.
- **Reflect Often:** At the end of each week, ask yourself, "What did I learn this week? How did I handle challenges?" This reflection keeps you aware of your mindset.
- **Embrace Small Wins:** Celebrate small improvements. This reminds you that growth is happening, even if it's not huge yet.

Changing your mindset isn't always easy. It involves catching negative thoughts and replacing them with more supportive ones. But with regular practice, these beliefs can become second nature, and you'll find that handling challenges and failure feels less terrifying and more like a natural part of growing.

Section 6: Real-Life Examples of Growth Through Failure

Sometimes it helps to see how others have turned their challenges and failures into stepping stones for success. Here are some brief examples:

1. **J.K. Rowling:** Before she became famous for the "Harry Potter" series, Rowling faced multiple rejections from publishers. She was also a single mother struggling to make ends meet. Many publishers turned down her manuscript, but she kept sending it out. Eventually, one publisher accepted it, and the series became a global success story. Rowling's repeated failures did not stop her; they encouraged her to keep trying.
2. **Michael Jordan:** Arguably one of the greatest basketball players of all time, Michael Jordan once said he failed over and over again, which is why he succeeded. In high school, he was cut from the varsity team, which fueled his drive to practice harder. He turned that disappointment into motivation, eventually becoming an NBA legend.
3. **Walt Disney:** Early in his career, Disney faced bankruptcy and saw several of his businesses fail. He was even fired from a newspaper job because they thought he "lacked imagination." Yet he continued to pursue his creative visions. Today, the Disney brand is known around the world for its animations, theme parks, and stories.
4. **Sara Blakely (Founder of Spanx):** She failed at multiple jobs before inventing the product that made her a billionaire. She sold fax machines door-to-door and tried different ventures. She says that her father encouraged her to fail by asking at the dinner table, "What did you fail at today?" This made her see failure as a normal step toward success.

5. **Albert Einstein:** Early in life, Einstein's teachers thought he was slow because he spoke very little as a child. He later failed the entrance exam to a polytechnic school on his first try. However, he kept studying and eventually passed. He went on to develop groundbreaking theories in physics that changed how we understand the universe.

In all these examples, failure wasn't the end. It was a turning point—a moment when these individuals decided to learn from their mistakes and keep going. They are living proof that failure can lead to success if we approach it with determination and a willingness to adapt.

Section 7: Supporting Others Through Their Challenges

As you grow more comfortable with facing your own challenges and failures, you may find opportunities to help others do the same. Supporting friends, family members, or coworkers in tough times not only helps them but can also reinforce your own positive mindset. Here are some ways to be supportive:

1. **Listen Actively:** Sometimes people just need to talk about their problems. Show them you're listening by asking follow-up questions and summarizing what they've said. Avoid jumping to solutions right away—just being heard can be a huge relief.
2. **Offer Empathy, Not Pity:** Empathy means trying to understand how the other person feels. Pity can make them feel small or ashamed. Instead of saying, "Oh, that's so sad, poor you," say, "I'm really sorry you're going through this. That sounds tough."
3. **Share Your Experiences:** If you've gone through a similar challenge or failure, it might help to share how you dealt with it. Hearing that someone else made it through can offer hope. Be careful not to make the conversation all about you, though—keep it brief and relevant.
4. **Encourage Growth Mindset:** Remind them that failure is not a permanent label. Praise their effort, creativity, or perseverance. If

they say things like "I'm no good at this," suggest adding "yet" at the end. Let them know their skills can improve over time with practice.
5. **Suggest Resources:** If appropriate, point them to helpful tools, like tutorials, books, or people who can offer expert advice. Sometimes, we struggle simply because we don't know where to turn for help.
6. **Celebrate Small Wins With Them:** When they make progress or learn something new, acknowledge it. Celebrating even small victories can boost motivation and confidence. It reminds them that they are moving forward, little by little.
7. **Know Your Limits:** You can be supportive, but you can't solve someone else's problems for them. If the issue is serious—like a mental health crisis—encourage them to speak to a professional counselor, therapist, or doctor. Your role is to support, not to replace professional help.

By being there for others, you strengthen your own resilience too. Each time you help someone, you're reminded that challenges and failures are part of life for everyone. It becomes clearer that facing these obstacles isn't a sign of weakness but a universal human experience that can bring people closer together.

Chapter 8: Learning from Others

Introduction

No one grows alone. Even the most independent person learns from other people—through books, classes, conversations, or simple observations. By looking at how others think and act, we can gain new insights, avoid common mistakes, and sometimes find the inspiration we need to keep going.

In this chapter, we'll explore the many ways you can learn from those around you. We'll talk about seeking out mentors, picking good role models, and even learning from peers who share your goals and challenges. We'll also discuss how to be open to advice and feedback, while staying true to your own path. Learning from others doesn't mean copying them exactly; it means taking the best parts of their knowledge and applying them to your life in a way that fits you.

By the end of this chapter, you'll see that you're surrounded by potential teachers—friends, colleagues, family, community members, and even strangers you meet online. The world is full of lessons if you know where to look. Whether you're trying to master a skill, explore a career, or simply become a kinder person, the experiences of others can guide you. Let's dive in and discover how to make the most of the wisdom and support that's already out there.

Section 1: Why Learning from Others Matters

We often think of learning as something that happens in a classroom with a teacher. But in reality, we can learn from almost anyone, in many different ways. Here are some reasons why learning from others is so valuable:

1. **Save Time and Effort:** If you want to learn a new skill—like playing guitar—finding someone who's already good at it can speed up your progress. They can show you the proper techniques, tell you what not to do, and recommend resources that worked for them. This saves you from random trial and error.
2. **Gain Multiple Perspectives:** Each person sees the world in a slightly different way. By listening to different perspectives, you expand your own thinking. You might discover a method or approach that you'd never have considered on your own. This can spark creativity and help you solve problems.
3. **Encouragement and Motivation:** It's easier to stay motivated when you see someone who's gone down the same path and succeeded. Their story can inspire you to keep going. Sometimes, just knowing that a certain achievement is possible can help you believe in your own potential.
4. **Community and Support:** Humans are social beings. Having people around you who share your interests or goals can create a support system. If you struggle, they can offer a listening ear or practical tips. If you succeed, they can celebrate with you. This community feeling makes the journey more enjoyable.
5. **Accountability:** When you learn together with others or share your progress, you're more likely to keep up the effort. For instance, if you join a writing group, you might meet weekly to discuss your latest pages. This regular check-in can push you to write more consistently than you would on your own.
6. **Real-World Application:** While books and videos are helpful, people with real-world experience can share stories about how things work in practical settings. For example, a professional chef can show you cooking techniques that might not appear in a basic recipe. A seasoned entrepreneur can explain common pitfalls in starting a business.

In short, we learn faster, stay motivated, and solve problems better when we draw on the knowledge and support of others. You don't have to reinvent the wheel or do everything by yourself. By opening up to lessons that people around you can offer—whether they're experts, peers, or even younger folks with fresh ideas—you give yourself a powerful edge in personal growth.

Section 2: Finding and Working with Mentors

A mentor is someone who has experience in a particular area and is willing to guide you. Mentors can be teachers, older relatives, experienced coworkers, or community leaders. The mentor-mentee relationship often involves regular meetings or conversations where the mentor offers advice, feedback, and encouragement.

How to Find a Mentor

1. **Look in Your Community:** Schools, churches, community centers, or local organizations often have experienced individuals who are open to mentoring.
2. **Ask Around:** Sometimes, a friend or family member knows someone who has the skills you want. A simple introduction could lead to a mentoring relationship.
3. **Use Online Platforms:** LinkedIn or other professional networks can help you find people in your field of interest. Reach out politely with a clear reason for why you'd value their mentorship.

Approaching a Potential Mentor

- **Be Clear About Your Goals:** Mentors appreciate knowing what you hope to achieve. Are you looking for career advice? Help with a hobby? Guidance in leadership skills?
- **Show Respect for Their Time:** Mentors are often busy. Explain how often you'd like to meet (such as once a month for a coffee chat or video call). Keep conversations focused and concise.
- **Be Prepared:** If you have specific questions or challenges, have them ready so the mentor can offer targeted advice.

Making the Most of Mentorship

1. **Be Open to Feedback:** A mentor might point out areas for improvement that you haven't considered. Receiving this feedback positively shows maturity.
2. **Take Action:** If your mentor gives you suggestions, try them out. Mentors feel motivated to keep helping when they see you applying their advice.
3. **Keep Them Updated:** Mentors want to know how you're doing. Even a quick email or message about your progress can make them feel appreciated.
4. **Show Gratitude:** A thank-you note or a small gesture of appreciation can go a long way in maintaining a good relationship.

Different Types of Mentors

- **Career Mentor:** Helps with job-related skills and decisions.
- **Skills Mentor:** Focuses on teaching you a specific ability—like coding, art, or cooking.
- **Life Mentor:** Guides you on broader personal growth, such as building confidence or work-life balance.

Remember, mentorship is a two-way street. While your mentor is guiding you, you should also respect their time, show kindness, and be willing to learn. The more effort you put into the relationship, the more you'll gain.

Section 3: Role Models vs. Mentors

People sometimes confuse the terms "mentor" and "role model," but they're not exactly the same thing:

- **Mentor:** Someone who works with you directly, offering advice and feedback, often in a personal, one-on-one context.
- **Role Model:** Someone you look up to for inspiration. You might follow their work, read about their life, or watch their interviews, but you might not have direct contact with them.

Both mentors and role models can help you grow, but in different ways.

Learning from Role Models

1. **Observe Their Habits and Traits:** Role models show us a possible path. For example, if you admire a famous athlete's work ethic, you can try to model your training after theirs. If you admire a humanitarian's kindness, you can look for ways to volunteer or serve others.
2. **Study Their Journey:** Many successful people share their stories in biographies, interviews, or blogs. These stories often include failures, doubts, and turning points. Reading about how they overcame obstacles can give you ideas for your own life.
3. **Adapt, Don't Copy:** While it's tempting to do exactly what your role model did, remember that their circumstances might differ from yours. You can learn the principles—like persistence, creativity, or empathy—and apply them in a way that suits your own situation.
4. **Multiple Role Models:** You don't have to limit yourself to one role model. You might admire someone's business sense, another person's artistic skill, and a third person's compassionate nature. Combining influences from various role models can give you a balanced approach to life.

When to Seek Mentorship Instead

If you need personal feedback or detailed guidance, a mentor is usually more helpful than a distant role model. For instance, if you're trying to master a specific skill—like writing code or playing an instrument—a mentor can watch your attempts and correct mistakes in real time. A role model may be an inspiration, but they might not be available to give you direct input.

Making Role Models a Part of Your Growth

- **Keep a Journal of Lessons Learned:** When you read about a role model's life or watch their interviews, note the key lessons and try to put them into practice.

- **Stay Curious:** If your role model overcame a big challenge, ask yourself what tools or mindset they used. Could you develop similar tools in your life?
- **Stay Realistic:** Recognize that role models are human, too. They have flaws and sometimes make mistakes. Don't be discouraged if you can't reach their level right away or if you discover they have faults. Focus on the positive traits that help you grow.

In summary, both mentors and role models can light the way for your development. A mentor gives you hands-on support, while a role model offers inspiration from a distance. Using both resources can help you become the best version of yourself.

Section 4: Peer Learning and Collaboration

Sometimes, we imagine that only experts can teach us. But our peers—people at a similar level—can be just as valuable. Peer learning happens when two or more people of roughly the same skill or knowledge level help each other grow.

Benefits of Peer Learning

1. **Shared Experiences:** Peers often face similar challenges at the same time. By discussing these challenges, you can swap tips and learn from each other's mistakes.
2. **Supportive Environment:** Peers understand your struggles firsthand because they're going through them, too. This can create a comforting atmosphere where everyone feels safe to admit confusion or ask questions.
3. **Teaching to Learn:** When you explain a concept to someone else, you deepen your own understanding. This is why study groups can be so effective—teaching is a powerful form of learning.

Examples of Peer Learning

- **Study Groups:** Classmates gather to review lessons, work on projects, or prepare for tests.
- **Coding Circles:** Programmers of similar levels share code, debug each other's work, or collaborate on small projects.
- **Writers' Workshops:** Writers read and critique each other's pieces, helping to refine writing style and clarity.
- **Language Exchange:** Two people learning each other's languages practice speaking together, each acting as both student and teacher.

Making Peer Learning Work

1. **Set Clear Goals:** If you form a group to learn something, agree on what you want to accomplish. For instance, a weekly study goal or a monthly project deadline.
2. **Create a Routine:** Meet regularly—whether in person or online—to maintain consistency. It could be once a week or twice a month.
3. **Encourage Openness:** Make sure all members feel comfortable sharing difficulties or admitting they don't understand something. A judgment-free zone is key to effective peer learning.
4. **Divide Tasks:** If you're collaborating on a project, assign roles or tasks based on each person's strengths. This ensures everyone contributes and learns.
5. **Celebrate Group Wins:** When the group reaches a milestone—like finishing a group project or scoring well on a test—take a moment to celebrate. This boosts group morale.

Balancing Peer Learning with Expert Input

While peer learning is great, it can also help to seek expert advice or mentorship from time to time. If the group gets stuck on a major issue, bringing in an experienced teacher or professional for guidance can break the deadlock. Think of it as combining the best of both worlds: the closeness and mutual support of peer learning with occasional expert insight to handle tricky problems.

Peer learning is a powerful method that keeps you motivated, sharpens your communication skills, and reminds you that you're not alone in facing challenges. By working together, you and your peers can lift each other up and achieve goals more efficiently.

Section 5: How to Receive Advice and Feedback

Learning from others often involves getting advice or feedback. But receiving feedback can be tricky, especially if it's about something personal—like your creative work, your performance at a job, or your behavior. Here are some guidelines to make the process smoother:

1. **Keep an Open Mind:** When someone gives feedback, resist the urge to defend yourself immediately. Even if you disagree, let them finish. There might be something valuable in their viewpoint.
2. **Ask Clarifying Questions:** If something isn't clear, politely ask for examples. For instance, "Could you show me which part of my presentation was confusing?" or "What specific changes do you suggest for my design?" Detailed feedback is more helpful than vague statements.
3. **Separate the Feedback from the Person:** Remember that feedback is about the task or the performance, not about your worth as a human being. If you feel attacked, step back and focus on what they're pointing out, not how they're saying it.
4. **Decide What to Accept:** Not all advice is good advice. Consider the source's expertise and motives. If the feedback makes sense and comes from a place of knowledge or care, it's likely worth acting on. If it seems off-base or poorly explained, it's okay to set it aside.
5. **Say Thank You:** Even if the feedback stings, the person offering it likely spent time thinking about how to help you. Thank them for their effort and let them know you'll consider their points.
6. **Reflect and Plan:** After receiving feedback, take some time to reflect. How can you use these insights to improve? Make a plan to apply the feedback in your next attempt, whether it's revising your work or practicing a new technique.

Handling Negative or Harsh Feedback

Sometimes, feedback can come across as negative or harsh. It might feel like an attack on your abilities. In these situations:

- **Stay Calm:** Take a deep breath. Getting defensive or angry usually ends the conversation without learning anything.
- **Look for the Gem:** There might be a "gem" of truth hidden in the harshness. Focus on that, rather than the negative tone.
- **Politely Set Boundaries:** If the feedback is rude or abusive, it's okay to say something like, "I appreciate your input, but can we keep the conversation respectful?"
- **Move On:** If the person is unwilling to provide constructive feedback, you may choose not to seek their input in the future.

By learning how to gracefully receive advice and feedback, you open the door to continuous improvement. Every piece of feedback is a chance to learn something new or spot an issue you might have overlooked. Over time, this skill will serve you well in school, work, relationships, and personal projects.

Section 6: Learning from Difficult People and Situations

Sometimes, the most challenging people or situations can offer valuable lessons. This might be a strict boss, a critical teacher, or a coworker you clash with. While it's not fun dealing with them, there can still be something to learn:

1. **Patience and Tolerance:** Handling difficult personalities can teach you how to stay calm under stress. You learn to pick your battles and avoid needless arguments.
2. **Better Communication:** A tough person might force you to communicate more clearly. You might have to find ways to say what you mean without provoking them. Over time, this polishes your communication skills.

3. **Self-Awareness:** Sometimes, a difficult situation reveals triggers or flaws in our own behavior. If you notice you always react defensively to a certain comment, you can work on that trait in yourself.
4. **Alternative Strategies:** If your usual methods don't work with a difficult person, you might have to try something different. This pushes you to innovate and adapt—useful skills in any area of life.
5. **Boundaries and Assertiveness:** Learning from others doesn't mean letting them walk all over you. Setting healthy boundaries is part of personal growth. A difficult person might teach you the importance of saying "no" or standing up for yourself when needed.

How to Extract Lessons from Tough Situations

- **Ask What You Can Control:** You can't always change another person's behavior, but you can control your own reactions. Focus on what you can do differently next time.
- **Look for Patterns:** Do you encounter similar problems with different people? If so, there might be a pattern in your approach or your environment that needs adjusting.
- **Seek External Perspective:** If you're truly stuck, talk to a friend or mentor about what's happening. A neutral viewpoint can help you see solutions you overlooked.

Balancing Learning with Well-Being

While it's true we can learn from difficult people, don't force yourself to stay in a harmful or toxic environment. If someone is abusive or consistently disrespectful, you might need to distance yourself. Learning is good, but protecting your mental and emotional well-being is essential.

Difficult people and tough situations can feel like obstacles in the short term, but they might also be stepping stones toward greater emotional intelligence and resilience. By approaching them as learning opportunities, you convert a stressful experience into a growth experience.

Section 7: Continuous Learning Through Books, Media, and Online Resources

Another way to learn from others—beyond personal contacts—is through the vast world of books, videos, podcasts, and online courses. The internet offers more information than ever before in history. Properly used, it can be a powerful tool for personal growth.

Books

1. **Nonfiction:** Biographies, self-help books, and instructional guides provide insights into topics ranging from history to personal finance.
2. **Fiction:** Novels can teach you about human nature, empathy, and different perspectives. Great stories often contain lessons in problem-solving and resilience.
3. **Reading Strategies:** Take notes, highlight passages, or discuss the book with friends to deepen your understanding.

Online Courses and Tutorials

- **Platforms Like Coursera or Khan Academy:** Offer free or low-cost lessons on subjects like math, coding, art, or business.
- **Professional Training Sites:** Some are specialized for certain fields—like cooking or graphic design.
- **Short Tutorials:** YouTube has countless channels dedicated to teaching skills—from fixing a computer to learning a new dance.

Podcasts and Webinars

- **Podcasts:** Many experts share their knowledge through weekly podcast episodes. You can learn while commuting, exercising, or doing chores.
- **Webinars and Live Streams:** Interactive live events let you ask questions and get answers in real-time.

Choosing Quality Content

With so much information available, it's crucial to pick reliable sources. Look for reviews, check the credentials of the author or instructor, and compare multiple sources if possible. Some people might claim to be experts without solid evidence.

Building a Personal Learning Schedule

To get the most out of these resources, create a routine:

1. **Set a Time:** Decide when you'll watch tutorials or read—perhaps 30 minutes each morning.
2. **Take Notes or Practice:** Simply watching or listening might not be enough. Try the exercises or outline the main points.
3. **Apply What You Learn:** Whenever possible, turn new knowledge into action. If you watch a cooking tutorial, attempt the recipe the same week. If you read a personal finance book, try the budgeting tips right away.

Staying Balanced

While online resources are fantastic, be mindful of internet overload. Sometimes, you can end up watching countless videos but never applying what you learn. Balance your screen time with real-life practice or offline reflection.

In today's digital world, you can access a wealth of knowledge anytime. By using these tools wisely, you can keep learning from people across the globe without leaving your home. Combine this with personal interactions, and you'll have a well-rounded approach to learning from others.

Section 8: Giving Back—Becoming a Teacher or Mentor Yourself

Learning from others is crucial, but there comes a time when you can also teach or mentor people who are less experienced than you. This doesn't mean you have to be an official "expert." You just need to be a bit further along the path than someone else.

Why Teach or Mentor?

1. **Deepen Your Understanding:** Teaching forces you to organize your thoughts. It helps you realize gaps in your own knowledge because your student's questions might stump you.
2. **Improve Communication Skills:** Explaining ideas clearly is a valuable skill in any career or relationship.
3. **Boost Confidence:** Seeing that you can help someone else succeed can make you feel more confident in your own abilities.
4. **Create a Positive Cycle:** When you share knowledge freely, you contribute to a supportive community. People you help might later teach someone else.

Ways to Start

- **Offer Help Informally:** If a friend struggles with a subject you know well, volunteer to help them study.
- **Join a Program:** Many schools and community centers have tutoring or mentorship programs you can join.
- **Online Platforms:** If you're comfortable teaching a particular skill—like playing guitar, speaking Spanish, or coding—you might offer short lessons through online platforms or forums.

Being a Good Teacher or Mentor

1. **Listen First:** Understand the other person's goals, challenges, and preferred learning style.

2. **Encourage Questions:** A beginner might not know what to ask. Create a friendly environment where they feel safe admitting confusion.
3. **Give Constructive Feedback:** Point out mistakes gently and offer specific suggestions for improvement.
4. **Set Achievable Goals:** Break down tasks into small steps, celebrating each victory along the way.
5. **Stay Patient:** Remember how you felt when you were learning. Patience goes a long way in building trust and confidence.

Balancing Teaching and Learning

Even as a teacher or mentor, you never stop being a student. Keep challenging yourself to learn new things. This dual role—learning from those ahead of you and teaching those behind you—creates a continuous loop of growth. You build a deeper understanding of the material and refine your people skills.

By giving back, you not only help someone else but also reinforce the lessons in your own mind. Plus, it feels good to know you're making a positive difference. This positive feeling can motivate you to keep pushing forward on your own goals.

Chapter 9: Nurturing Positive Relationships

Introduction

Relationships play an important role in every part of life. Whether it's with family, friends, classmates, colleagues, or romantic partners, the relationships we have can affect how we feel each day. Positive relationships provide support, joy, and a sense of belonging. Negative or toxic relationships, on the other hand, can cause stress, sadness, and sometimes even harm our health.

In this chapter, we will explore what it means to nurture positive relationships. We'll look at how to build trust, communicate clearly, and be kind while still respecting our own boundaries. We'll also talk about empathy and understanding, which can help us connect more deeply with others. Conflict is normal in any relationship, so we'll discuss ways to resolve disagreements respectfully and find common ground.

By the end of this chapter, you'll have a toolbox of ideas for forming and maintaining healthy connections with the people in your life. You don't have to be perfect in every relationship—no one is. But with consistent care and attention, you can experience closer friendships, stronger family bonds, and happier interactions overall. When relationships are positive, life feels brighter, and it becomes easier to handle everyday challenges. Let's dive in and learn how to nurture the kinds of connections that enrich our lives.

Section 1: Understanding the Value of Positive Relationships

People are social creatures. We depend on one another for help, company, and emotional support. Here are some of the main ways positive relationships help us thrive:

1. **Emotional Support:** When you're feeling down or stressed, having a friend or family member who listens can make a huge difference. Sometimes, just knowing someone cares can lift your mood. You might feel lonely if you don't have supportive relationships, and loneliness can lead to sadness or health problems over time.
2. **Sense of Belonging:** Being part of a group—whether it's a circle of friends, a sports team, or a family—gives you a feeling that you're not alone. This sense of belonging satisfies a deep human need. It's comforting to know there are people who accept you as you are.
3. **Shared Experiences:** Life is more fun when you share experiences. Think about how a party feels more alive with friends around, or how a simple movie night is special when you watch together. Shared experiences create memories and deepen bonds.
4. **Personal Growth:** Good relationships challenge you to be better. Maybe a friend offers you a new perspective on a problem, or a family member encourages you to pursue a hobby you love. Interacting with others can inspire you to try new things, learn new skills, or change harmful habits.
5. **Better Health:** Research shows that people with strong social connections often live longer and are happier overall. Having friends or loved ones you can turn to can reduce stress levels. On the other hand, isolation can raise stress, which may lead to health issues. So your relationships can affect your body and mind.
6. **Help in Times of Need:** A strong support network can help you with big and small challenges—like moving to a new house, studying for a tough exam, dealing with an illness, or simply needing advice. You're more likely to succeed when you have people cheering you on or helping you out.

It's important to note that positive relationships don't just happen automatically. They take time, energy, and care. You might need to reach out, ask how someone is doing, or plan an activity together. Over time, these small steps add up. If you notice a relationship isn't providing these benefits—if it makes you feel stressed or upset more often than not—it might be worth re-evaluating or finding ways to improve it. Sometimes, adjusting communication patterns or setting new boundaries can turn a tense connection into a healthier one. Other times, it might be best to step away from toxic relationships altogether, especially if they involve constant negativity or harm. Understanding the value of positive connections is the first step toward cultivating them in your own life.

Section 2: Building Healthy Communication Skills

Communication is the heart of any relationship. It involves more than just talking; it includes listening, understanding the other person's perspective, and expressing yourself clearly. Here are some tips to help you build healthy communication skills:

1. **Be Clear and Direct:** When you talk to someone, say what you mean as simply as possible. If you're upset because a friend canceled plans at the last minute, let them know, politely: "I felt disappointed when you canceled. Can we plan another time to meet?" Avoid beating around the bush or making vague statements. Clear communication reduces confusion.
2. **Choose the Right Time and Place:** If you want to discuss something serious, find a time and place where both you and the other person can focus. Trying to talk about a sensitive issue in the middle of a noisy event or when someone is rushing out the door can lead to misunderstandings. Pick a calm environment or even schedule a dedicated moment to chat.
3. **Use "I" Statements:** Instead of saying, "You always do this," try saying, "I feel upset when this happens." This small shift makes a big difference. It focuses on how you feel rather than attacking the other person. For example, instead of "You never listen to me," say, "I feel ignored when you check your phone while I'm talking."
4. **Avoid Blame and Criticism:** Criticizing someone's character ("You're so lazy") often makes them defensive. Instead, address the specific action. For instance, "It bothers me when you don't finish your part of our group assignment" is more constructive. It points to the behavior, not the person.
5. **Keep Your Emotions in Check:** It's natural to feel angry or frustrated during conflict, but yelling or name-calling rarely helps. If you feel you're losing control, take a deep breath or ask for a short break. You can continue the conversation when you feel calmer.
6. **Be Open to Their Viewpoint:** Communication is a two-way street. Try to see the situation from the other person's perspective. Ask questions to understand their thoughts and feelings. Even if you

disagree, acknowledging their viewpoint shows respect and can defuse tension.
7. **Recognize Nonverbal Cues:** Body language, tone of voice, and facial expressions all convey meaning. Crossing your arms might show defensiveness, while nodding can show understanding. Pay attention to these signals, both in yourself and in others.

By practicing these communication skills, you set the stage for healthier, more respectful interactions. Good communication is like a bridge that connects you to another person, allowing you to understand each other and work through issues together. Over time, clear and caring communication builds trust, respect, and closeness—key elements of a positive relationship.

Section 3: The Art of Listening and Empathy

Talking is only half of communication; the other half is listening. It might sound simple, but truly listening can be surprisingly hard, especially when distractions are everywhere. Empathy, which is the ability to understand and share someone else's feelings, goes hand in hand with good listening. Together, they form a strong foundation for positive relationships.

Why Listening Matters

1. **Shows You Care:** When you give someone your full attention—putting away your phone, maintaining eye contact, nodding along—it tells them they matter. This simple act can make the other person feel respected and valued.
2. **Reduces Misunderstandings:** Half-listening can lead to missing key details or misinterpreting what someone means. Active listening helps you gather accurate information, reducing conflicts that arise from misunderstandings.
3. **Builds Trust:** If people notice you consistently listen to them, they'll be more likely to open up in the future. Trust grows when both sides feel heard and understood.

Tips for Active Listening

- **Focus on the Speaker:** Eliminate distractions. If possible, face the person speaking. If you're on the phone, pause other activities so you can concentrate.
- **Show Interest:** Use verbal cues like "I see," "Wow," or "Really?" to show you're following the story. Nonverbal cues like nodding, smiling, or leaning forward also signal engagement.
- **Paraphrase or Summarize:** After the person finishes speaking, try restating what they said in your own words: "So you're feeling upset because your teacher gave you a lower grade than you expected, right?" This helps confirm you understood them correctly.
- **Ask Clarifying Questions:** If something is unclear, politely ask for more details. For instance, "When you said you felt 'left out,' what exactly happened?"

Understanding Empathy

Empathy means stepping into someone else's shoes. It doesn't require you to fix their problems or feel their sadness exactly as they do, but it does mean acknowledging their feelings and letting them know you understand.

- **Listen Without Judgment:** If a friend is upset about something, let them express themselves before offering opinions. If you judge them right away, they might shut down.
- **Validate Their Emotions:** You can say things like, "That sounds really tough," or "I can see why you'd feel that way." Validation shows the other person their feelings are valid.
- **Relate When Appropriate:** If you've had a similar experience, briefly share it to show you truly get it. But be careful not to make the conversation all about you.

When someone feels empathized with, it can ease their emotional burden. They realize they're not alone, and that sense of being understood can strengthen your bond. Practicing listening and empathy might feel awkward at first, especially if you're used to quick, surface-level conversations. However, each time you truly listen and show genuine understanding, you build deeper, more meaningful connections. Over time, you'll find that people appreciate your care, and your relationships will become richer and more supportive.

Section 4: Setting Boundaries and Resolving Conflict

Even in the closest relationships, conflicts can arise. Disagreements are normal—they can happen over opinions, plans, or even small everyday habits. The key is learning to resolve these issues in a healthy way, which often involves setting clear boundaries. Boundaries tell people what is acceptable in terms of behavior, time, or personal space.

Why Boundaries Are Important

1. **Protects Your Well-Being:** Without boundaries, you might find yourself saying "yes" to too many commitments or tolerating actions that make you uncomfortable. This can lead to stress, resentment, or burnout.
2. **Respects Others' Autonomy:** Boundaries go both ways. Just as you have limits, other people have theirs. Recognizing and respecting their lines promotes mutual respect.
3. **Promotes Healthy Interaction:** When everyone understands each other's boundaries, it reduces confusion. People know what's okay and what's not, so they can avoid harmful or disrespectful behaviors.

Setting Boundaries

- **Identify Your Limits:** Think about what makes you feel safe, respected, and comfortable. Maybe you need alone time each day, or you don't like to discuss certain personal topics with casual acquaintances.
- **Communicate Firmly but Kindly:** Let the other person know your boundaries in a calm tone. For instance, "I need some quiet time

after work before we talk," or "I prefer not to share my private issues at work."
- **Follow Through:** If a boundary is crossed, gently remind the person. If they repeatedly ignore your limits, consider whether the relationship is healthy or if you need further steps to protect yourself.

Resolving Conflict Constructively

1. **Stay Calm:** Anger can make disagreements worse. If you feel your temper rising, take a break. You can say, "I need a moment to gather my thoughts."
2. **Listen to Each Other:** Each person should have a chance to explain their viewpoint without interruption. Returning to active listening can help prevent misunderstandings.
3. **Look for Common Ground:** Find an area where you both agree or at least understand each other's main concern. This shared viewpoint can be a starting point to build a solution.
4. **Suggest Solutions or Compromises:** If you want to decide who does chores, for example, you could propose a schedule. If you disagree about how much time to spend together, you could find a balance that respects both preferences.
5. **Apologize When Necessary:** If you realize you made a mistake or said something hurtful, an honest apology can go a long way. It shows that you respect the other person's feelings.
6. **Know When to Agree to Disagree:** Sometimes you won't see eye to eye, and that's okay. If the issue isn't critical, you can move on without having to convert the other person to your viewpoint.

Boundaries and conflict resolution are about respect—respect for yourself and respect for others. When disagreements arise, staying calm, listening well, and seeking mutual understanding can transform conflict into growth. Over time, practicing these skills can prevent small arguments from escalating and help maintain a positive, supportive environment in your relationships.

Section 5: Cultivating Trust and Respect

Trust and respect are two pillars of any strong relationship. Without trust, people feel guarded and suspicious. Without respect, they feel undervalued or disrespected. Both are essential for a stable, caring bond—be it with friends, family, or a partner.

Building Trust

1. **Keep Your Promises:** If you say you'll do something, do your best to follow through. Whether it's showing up on time or keeping a secret, reliability shows people they can count on you.
2. **Be Honest:** Even small lies can erode trust over time. Practice honesty in daily interactions. If you make a mistake, admit it rather than hiding or denying it. Honesty, even when uncomfortable, is crucial for deep trust.
3. **Respect Privacy:** If a friend confides in you, honor their confidence. Don't share their personal secrets without permission. When people realize you respect their privacy, they feel safer opening up.
4. **Give Trust as Well:** Trust is a two-way street. Show that you believe in the other person's integrity and abilities unless they give you a clear reason not to. This encourages them to trust you back.

Showing Respect

1. **Acknowledge Differences:** Everyone is unique. You don't have to agree with someone's preferences or beliefs to respect them. You can say, "I see we have different viewpoints, but I respect your right to your opinion."
2. **Use Polite Language:** Basic politeness—like saying "please," "thank you," and "excuse me"—creates a respectful tone. It might sound simple, but such gestures often carry a lot of meaning.
3. **Be Supportive:** Respect can also mean supporting someone's interests or goals. If a friend is learning a new skill, cheer them on or offer help if they want it. Show that you value their efforts.
4. **Avoid Insults or Put-Downs:** Even playful teasing can hurt if it hits a sensitive area. Keep your humor kind, and if someone seems uncomfortable, stop immediately.

Rebuilding Trust and Respect

Sometimes, trust or respect gets damaged—maybe you forgot a big promise or said something hurtful in anger. Rebuilding takes time:

- **Admit the Mistake:** Own up to what you did wrong. A sincere apology can start the healing process.
- **Show Consistency:** You'll need to consistently act in a trustworthy or respectful manner over time to prove you've changed.
- **Be Patient:** The other person might still feel cautious. It may take multiple positive interactions to fully regain their confidence.

When trust and respect form the base of your relationships, you can handle difficulties more smoothly. People feel safe to express themselves, and disagreements don't turn into personal attacks. Over time, a relationship grounded in trust and respect can deepen into a lasting connection that enriches both individuals' lives.

Section 6: Maintaining Relationships Over the Long Term

Forming a new friendship or connection can be exciting, but keeping it strong over the years requires ongoing effort. Whether it's a friendship, family bond, or romantic partnership, relationships evolve as people grow, change jobs, move to new places, or develop new interests. Here are ways to nurture these connections over time:

1. **Regular Check-Ins:** Life can get busy, and months can pass without communication. Make an effort to send a quick message, call, or meet up. Even a short "How are you doing?" can strengthen the bond and show you care.
2. **Shared Activities:** Doing things together fosters connection. This could mean going on a trip, playing a sport, or cooking a meal together. If you live far apart, consider doing an online activity, like a video chat game or a virtual watch party.

3. **Celebrate Milestones:** If a friend achieves something—a graduation, a new job, or a birthday—acknowledge it. A quick congratulatory note or planning a small get-together can show you're happy for their success.
4. **Adapt to Change:** People's schedules, interests, or priorities can shift. Stay open to new ways of spending time together. For example, if your friend used to love going to the gym but now prefers biking outdoors, join them for a bike ride occasionally. Flexibility helps maintain the bond.
5. **Manage Conflicts Quickly:** Small misunderstandings can grow if ignored. If something bothers you, address it calmly rather than letting resentment build up. Often, clearing the air strengthens the relationship.
6. **Respect Each Other's Growth:** Over the years, goals and dreams can change. You might want a certain career path while your friend chooses another. Encourage each other's growth, even if your paths differ. True friends and partners support each other's progress without demanding they stay the same.
7. **Quality Over Quantity:** Not all relationships need daily interaction. Some friends may talk once a week, while others check in monthly or less. What matters is the quality of the connection. Do you understand each other? Are you there for each other when it counts?
8. **Build New Memories:** While reminiscing about the past is fun, creating new shared moments keeps the relationship fresh. Plan future gatherings or new experiences to look forward to. This helps the relationship grow instead of staying stuck in old times.

Long-term relationships require patience, understanding, and continuous effort. They might not always be easy, especially when people face life changes. However, by staying in touch, being supportive, and resolving issues as they come, you can keep those precious bonds strong. In the end, maintaining close connections can bring comfort, joy, and a sense of belonging, making the journey through life richer and more meaningful.

Chapter 10: Managing Time and Energy

Introduction

We all have 24 hours in a day, but it often feels like there's never enough time. Between school, work, chores, hobbies, relationships, and rest, life can get busy. Managing your time well is crucial to achieving your goals and maintaining balance. Alongside time management, energy management is also essential. After all, even if you have a perfectly planned schedule, you can't do your tasks well if you're exhausted or burned out.

In this chapter, we will dive into practical ways to organize your day, set priorities, and fight procrastination. We'll also look at strategies to keep your mind and body energized, such as getting enough sleep and taking breaks. By combining good time management with smart energy management, you'll find that you can get more done without feeling overwhelmed. You'll also discover that you have more room for creativity, relaxation, and the positive relationships we discussed in the previous chapter.

By the end of Chapter 10, you'll have tools to plan your days effectively, handle unexpected changes, and stay motivated over the long run. You don't have to be perfect at scheduling or productivity—no one is. But with a few key techniques and a healthy approach to your energy levels, you can accomplish what matters most to you and still have time to enjoy life. Let's begin!

Section 1: Why Time Management Matters

Time management is not just about being busy; it's about making sure you spend your time in ways that align with your goals and values. Here's why it matters:

1. **Reduces Stress and Overwhelm:** When you have a plan, you're less likely to feel panicked by looming deadlines or a long to-do list. Instead of rushing last-minute, you can pace yourself and know you're on track.
2. **Improves Productivity:** With good time management, you can complete tasks more quickly and efficiently. You're less likely to waste hours on low-priority activities when you know what's important.
3. **Creates Space for Personal Interests:** Effective time management isn't just about work or school. It also frees up time for hobbies, exercise, socializing, or simply relaxing. This balance keeps you motivated and helps prevent burnout.
4. **Builds Self-Discipline and Confidence:** When you schedule your day and stick to it, you build discipline. Over time, seeing that you can accomplish tasks on schedule boosts your self-confidence and encourages you to aim higher.
5. **Ensures Deadlines Are Met:** Whether it's an assignment for school or a project for work, missing deadlines can cause problems. By planning, you can avoid last-minute rushes and the mistakes they often bring.
6. **Allows for Flexibility:** Ironically, having a plan can make you more flexible. If you know your top priorities, it's easier to rearrange tasks when unexpected events happen. You're also less likely to drop important responsibilities in a panic.

It's important to note that time management is personal. A method that works for one person may not work for another. Some like detailed hourly schedules, while others prefer broad weekly goals. The key is to find a system that keeps you focused but doesn't feel suffocating. Experimenting with different approaches can help you discover what fits your lifestyle.

Remember, good time management isn't about filling every minute with work. It's about making intentional choices so you can achieve your goals while also having room to rest and recharge. When you manage your time wisely, you gain more control over your life, leading to better results in school, work, and personal pursuits.

Section 2: Planning and Prioritization

To manage your time effectively, you need to plan what needs to be done and decide in what order it should be done. This is where prioritization comes in.

Identifying Your Priorities

1. **List All Your Tasks:** Start by writing down everything you need or want to do. This could include studying, chores, work assignments, exercise, hobbies, and social activities.
2. **Categorize Tasks:** Separate them into groups like "urgent," "important," and "less important." Urgent tasks have a close deadline, while important tasks have significant value—like studying for a major exam or preparing a big work project.
3. **Be Realistic:** Recognize that you have limited time. If you list 20 "most important" tasks for one day, you may set yourself up for failure. Focus on what truly matters.

The "Must-Should-Could" Method

A helpful way to organize tasks is to categorize them as Must, Should, and Could:

- **Must:** Tasks you absolutely must do today (e.g., finishing a school assignment that's due tomorrow).
- **Should**: Tasks that are important but not urgent, or tasks that can wait if absolutely necessary (e.g., cleaning your room).
- **Could:** Tasks that would be nice to do if you have extra time (e.g., practicing guitar for fun).

By sorting tasks this way, you get a clearer picture of what to tackle first.

Creating a Schedule

1. **Use a Calendar or Planner:** Whether it's a paper planner or a digital app, having a visual layout of your schedule helps you see deadlines and free slots.

2. **Time Blocking:** This involves setting aside specific blocks of time for certain tasks. For example, 8:00–9:00 AM for reading and responding to emails, 9:00–10:00 AM for working on a project, and so on.
3. **Add Buffers:** People often underestimate how long tasks will take. Include small buffers (like 5–15 minutes) between tasks. This gives you a cushion if something runs longer than expected.
4. **Review and Adjust:** Each evening or morning, review your schedule. If you didn't finish something, decide when you'll do it. If new tasks appear, see where they fit. Flexibility is key.

Staying Focused on the Plan

Even with a great plan, distractions can throw you off track. Turn off notifications when possible, or designate specific times to check messages. If you struggle to stay on task, try techniques like the Pomodoro method (working in 25-minute intervals followed by a short break).

By planning out your tasks and prioritizing them, you ensure that you spend your time on what truly matters. Over time, you'll find it easier to finish important work before deadlines and still enjoy fun activities or downtime. A clear plan keeps you from feeling scattered or overwhelmed, allowing you to move steadily toward your goals.

Section 3: Dealing with Procrastination

Procrastination is when you delay doing something important, usually by distracting yourself with easier or more enjoyable tasks. It can lead to stress, missed deadlines, or poor performance. Here are some strategies to help you beat procrastination:

1. **Understand Why You're Procrastinating:** Sometimes, you avoid a task because it feels too big or boring. Other times, you might be afraid of failing. Identifying the root cause can help you find the right solution.

2. **Break Tasks into Small Steps:** Large tasks can feel overwhelming. If you have a 10-page report to write, start with creating an outline, then write one page at a time. This makes the job more manageable and less scary.
3. **Set Short Deadlines or Use Timers:** Instead of saying, "I'll work on this all day," commit to just 20 or 30 minutes of focused work. Use a timer if that helps. Once you start, you might find it's not as bad as you feared and keep going.
4. **Reward Yourself:** Giving yourself something to look forward to can motivate you. Promise yourself a break, a snack, or a brief scroll through social media after you complete a specific chunk of work. Just be sure to keep these rewards short so you don't get sidetracked for too long.
5. **Remove Distractions:** If your phone is a major distraction, put it on silent or leave it in another room. If you can't resist browsing the internet aimlessly, consider using website blockers that limit access to certain sites for a set time.
6. **Find an Accountability Partner:** Tell a friend or family member about your goal. For example, "I will finish the first draft of my essay by 5 PM." Having someone check on your progress can give you an extra push to stay on track.
7. **Visualize the Outcome:** Sometimes, thinking about how good it will feel to have the task done can motivate you to start. Remind yourself of the benefits of completing your work—like less stress and better results.
8. **Aim for Progress, Not Perfection:** Procrastination can stem from fear of not doing a job perfectly. Tell yourself it's okay to do it imperfectly at first. You can always edit or improve later. The key is to begin.

Procrastination is common, but it doesn't have to control your life. By understanding why you delay tasks and applying these techniques, you can train yourself to start sooner. Over time, you'll see that taking small steps forward consistently is more effective than waiting for the "right moment" or a burst of motivation that may never come. Breaking free from procrastination leads to better results and less stress.

Section 4: Techniques for Productivity

Beyond avoiding procrastination, there are proven methods to boost your productivity—enabling you to accomplish tasks more effectively and free up time for relaxation or hobbies. Here are some popular techniques:

1. **Pomodoro Technique:** Work in short bursts (often 25 minutes), then take a 5-minute break. After 4 work sessions, take a longer break of 15-20 minutes. This method helps you stay focused and prevents burnout. Use a timer to stick to it strictly.
2. **Eisenhower Matrix:** Named after President Dwight D. Eisenhower, this tool sorts tasks into four categories:
    - **Urgent and Important** (do these first),
    - **Important but Not Urgent** (schedule these),
    - **Urgent but Not Important** (delegate or reduce them),
    - **Neither Important nor Urgent** (limit or remove these).
    This matrix guides you to prioritize tasks that really matter while reducing time on trivial tasks.
3. **Batching Similar Tasks:** Group tasks of the same nature together. For instance, set aside one block of time to respond to emails and another block to make phone calls. Switching between different types of tasks can break your flow, so batching keeps you in the zone.
4. **2-Minute Rule:** If a task takes less than 2 minutes—like sending a quick email reply—do it immediately. This prevents small tasks from piling up and cluttering your to-do list.
5. **Set Clear Goals:** Whether for a day, a week, or a month, having specific goals helps you target your energy. Instead of vaguely saying, "I want to exercise more," define a goal like, "I will jog for 20 minutes, three times this week." This clarity aids motivation.
6. **Time Audits:** Sometimes, we lose track of time without realizing it. For a week, note how you spend each hour of the day. You might discover you spend a lot of time on social media or TV. Once you see the pattern, you can adjust to allocate more time to meaningful tasks.
7. **Plan for Breaks and Downtime:** Counterintuitive as it might sound, scheduling breaks can make you more productive. Knowing you

have a break coming up lets you focus during work intervals, and the rest helps recharge your energy.
8. **Review at the End of the Day:** Take a few minutes to see what you accomplished. Did you meet your goals? If not, why? This reflection helps you improve your approach for the next day.

These techniques aren't one-size-fits-all. Try a few and see which ones suit your personality and lifestyle. The goal is to increase effectiveness, not to turn yourself into a machine. A good productivity system should help you achieve more while maintaining balance in your life.

Section 5: Balancing Activities

Managing time isn't just about doing more work; it's about creating a harmonious balance among various life areas—like school or work responsibilities, personal interests, relationships, and health. Here's how to ensure you don't tip the scales too far in any one direction:

1. **Identify Core Life Areas:** These might include education, career, family, friends, health (physical and mental), hobbies, and community involvement. Recognize that each area plays a role in your overall well-being.
2. **Allocate Time Intentionally:** Decide how much time you want to spend in each area. For instance, if family time is very important to you, schedule activities or dinners with family so they become a non-negotiable part of your week.
3. **Use a Weekly View:** Instead of trying to cram everything into a single day, look at your week as a whole. Maybe weekdays are busy with work or school, so you reserve weekends for relaxing or social events. A bigger view can help you see patterns and plan for them.
4. **Avoid Overcommitment:** Saying "yes" to everything can lead to burnout. Sometimes, turning down an extra project or invitation is the best choice if you're already stretched thin. Politely decline and explain you want to maintain a healthy balance.
5. **Schedule Fun and Rest:** While it might sound odd to plan fun, putting it on your calendar ensures you make time for it. Watching

a favorite show, going out with friends, or indulging in a hobby can refresh your mind. Adequate sleep also needs a place in your schedule—lack of rest can severely hurt your effectiveness.
6. **Be Adaptable:** Life circumstances change—maybe you get a new job, start a family, or shift your career goals. Whenever your priorities change, revisit your schedule and adjust. Don't stick to an old plan that no longer fits your reality.
7. **Quality Over Quantity:** Spending a lot of time with friends doesn't always mean you're building closer relationships. Sometimes a shorter, but more focused hangout can be more meaningful than hours of halfhearted interaction. Apply this idea to other areas, too—quality study sessions often beat hours of distracted studying.
8. **Reflect Regularly:** Ask yourself monthly or quarterly if you're still satisfied with how you're spending your time. Are you feeling overwhelmed or neglecting something important? Adjust your balance as needed.

A balanced life is not about achieving perfect equality every day—it's about making sure no single area takes over your life for too long. By balancing activities, you maintain your well-being and keep your motivation high. You'll find it easier to stay committed to your responsibilities when you also make room for enjoyment, relationships, and self-care.

Section 6: Managing Energy Levels

Even the best time management plans fail if you're constantly fatigued or stressed. Your energy level is the fuel that powers you through your tasks. Here's how to manage it effectively:

Physical Health

1. **Quality Sleep:** Aim for 7–9 hours of sleep each night (or more if you're a teenager). Consistent bedtimes and wake-up times can help regulate your body clock. Lack of sleep leads to poor focus, mood swings, and reduced productivity.

2. **Balanced Diet:** Eating wholesome foods like fruits, vegetables, whole grains, and lean proteins provides steady energy. Too much sugar or junk food can cause energy spikes followed by crashes. Staying hydrated also supports clear thinking.
3. **Regular Exercise:** Physical activity, even a short walk, can boost your mood and energy. Exercise improves blood circulation, which helps you feel more alert. It also releases endorphins—chemicals in your brain that make you feel good.

Mental and Emotional Health

1. **Take Breaks:** If you work or study for hours without rest, mental fatigue sets in. Short breaks—where you step away from your desk, stretch, or take a few deep breaths—can recharge your mind.
2. **Relaxation Techniques:** Activities like meditation, gentle yoga, or even coloring can help relieve stress and calm your mind. Less stress translates to more available energy for meaningful tasks.
3. **Positive Relationships:** As we discussed in Chapter 9, supportive relationships can boost your emotional well-being. Feeling lonely or dealing with conflicts drains energy, while positive connections can uplift you.

Mindset and Motivation

1. **Set Meaningful Goals:** Working on tasks that align with your personal values or interests can keep your energy high. If you see a purpose in what you're doing, motivation naturally rises.
2. **Celebrate Small Wins:** Recognizing small achievements can renew your enthusiasm. A quick "Good job!" to yourself or sharing your success with a friend can give you a surge of positive energy.
3. **Avoid Perfectionism:** Striving for perfect results in every task can exhaust you mentally. Aim to do your best within reasonable limits. Continuous progress is more sustainable than chasing unrealistic standards.

Creating an Energy-Friendly Routine

- **Morning Rituals:** Start your day with something positive—like a brief walk, a healthy breakfast, or a few minutes of quiet reflection. This can set a calm, energetic tone for the day.
- **Midday Check-In:** Around lunchtime, notice how you feel. Are you tired, hungry, or stressed? Adjust your afternoon accordingly—maybe take a quick break or have a small snack.
- **Wind-Down Routine:** In the evening, avoid bright screens before bed and do relaxing activities like reading or stretching. This signals your body that it's time to rest.

By caring for both your body and mind, you create the energy you need to tackle your daily tasks. Good time management combined with balanced energy levels means you can work smarter, not just harder. Over time, this approach allows you to sustain your efforts without burning out. When your energy is stable, you'll likely find your mood is better, your mind is sharper, and you're more able to enjoy both work and leisure activities.

Chapter 11: Strengthening Self-Confidence

Introduction

Self-confidence is the belief that you can handle challenges, learn new things, and succeed in what you set out to do. A confident person does not necessarily believe they are perfect; rather, they trust that they can grow and improve over time. Having self-confidence can make a big difference in everyday life. It can help you speak up in class, try out for a sports team, make new friends, or pursue a hobby without worrying too much about what people think.

In this chapter, we will explore many aspects of self-confidence: how it develops, what obstacles can get in the way, and how to build it up if you feel low or insecure. We'll talk about changing negative thoughts, stepping out of your comfort zone, and celebrating your achievements—big and small. You'll discover that confidence is not something you are simply born with; it's a skill you can learn.

By the end of this chapter, you will have practical strategies for believing in your own abilities. You'll see that self-confidence grows when you face your fears, learn from mistakes, and give yourself credit for your efforts. Remember that everyone struggles with self-confidence at times, but with patience and practice, you can become more sure of yourself and live a richer, more fulfilling life.

Section 1: Understanding Self-Confidence

What Is Self-Confidence?

Self-confidence is the feeling or belief that you can face life's tasks and challenges without constantly doubting yourself. You trust that you have some ability or the potential to develop it. This does not mean you think you're the best at everything. Rather, you believe in your capacity to learn, adapt, and keep trying, even when things are tough.

The Difference Between Self-Confidence and Arrogance

Self-confidence can sometimes be confused with arrogance or boasting. Arrogance means thinking you're better than everyone else. A confident person, however, doesn't need to brag or put others down. They simply believe in their own value while also respecting other people. True confidence often comes with humility: you recognize your strengths but also know there's always room to grow.

Why Self-Confidence Matters

1. **Better Performance:** When you believe you can do something, you often try harder and persist longer. This can lead to better results—like doing well on a test or performing your best in a sports match.
2. **Healthier Relationships:** A confident person is usually more comfortable communicating honestly with friends or family. They are less afraid to share their opinions or feelings, which can lead to more genuine, supportive relationships.
3. **Greater Resilience:** Confidence includes the understanding that failure is not the end. If you believe you can figure things out or improve, you'll bounce back more quickly after mistakes or disappointments.
4. **Happier Mindset:** Constant self-doubt can lead to anxiety or sadness. While everyone worries sometimes, a confident person is more likely to think positively about the future and maintain a calmer outlook.

Factors That Affect Self-Confidence

- **Early Experiences:** If you grew up in an environment where people regularly criticized you, you might struggle with low self-confidence. If you received support and encouragement, you may find it easier to trust in your abilities.

- **Past Achievements or Failures:** Successes can boost your confidence, while failures—especially if not handled well—can damage it. However, failures can also become a source of growth if you learn from them.
- **Social Comparisons:** Constantly comparing yourself to others (especially on social media) can hurt your self-confidence. You might forget that people usually show only their highlights online, not their struggles.
- **Personality Traits:** Some people are naturally more outgoing and self-assured, while others are shy or cautious. Either way, confidence can be developed with practice.

Understanding what self-confidence really is—and what it is not—lays the groundwork for building it. You don't have to become perfect to feel confident. You just need to believe that you can grow, adapt, and handle life's ups and downs. As you read on, you'll see that there are many tools and habits that can nurture this belief within you.

Section 2: Overcoming Negative Thoughts and Self-Doubt

Even the most confident people sometimes face negative thoughts that say, "You're not good enough," or "You're going to fail." This self-doubt can hold you back from trying new things or enjoying life. Overcoming these thoughts is a key step in growing your self-confidence.

Recognizing Negative Self-Talk

First, it helps to notice when you're being overly critical of yourself. These thoughts might sound like:

- "I'm so stupid."
- "I always mess up."
- "Nobody likes me."
- "I'll fail, so there's no point in trying."

When you catch these thoughts, ask yourself if they're based on facts or just assumptions. Often, they're exaggerated. Maybe you made a mistake, but that doesn't mean you "always" mess up or that you're "stupid." Identifying these thought patterns is the first step to challenging them.

Challenging Negative Thoughts

1. **Look for Evidence:** Is it really true that you "always" fail? Probably not. You've likely succeeded at some tasks. Listing those successes can help you see the bigger picture.
2. **Reframe the Thought:** Instead of "I can't do this," say, "I can't do this yet, but I can learn." Adding "yet" reminds you that skills develop over time.
3. **Imagine a Friend:** If your friend was in your situation, would you say these negative things to them? Probably not. Treat yourself with the same kindness you'd offer someone you care about.

Building Positive Self-Talk

Replace negative thoughts with supportive, realistic statements:

- "I'm doing my best, and that's good enough."
- "Mistakes are part of learning."
- "I have succeeded before, so I can succeed again."
- "Even if I fail, I'll gain experience and try again."

This isn't about lying to yourself or ignoring real problems. It's about acknowledging reality while also recognizing your ability to improve.

Dealing with Fear of Failure

A big part of self-doubt is the fear of making mistakes or failing. One helpful approach is to ask, "What's the worst that could happen if I fail?" Often, the worst-case scenario isn't as horrible as you imagine. You might feel embarrassed or have to try again, but life usually goes on. Facing this possibility can reduce the power fear has over you.

Seek Support

If negative thoughts feel overwhelming, it can help to talk to a trusted friend, family member, or counselor. Sometimes an outside perspective can help you see that you're being too hard on yourself.

Overcoming negative thoughts and self-doubt is an ongoing process. You might still feel nervous or unsure sometimes—that's normal. But as you practice catching and challenging unhelpful thoughts, you'll gradually build a stronger, more confident mindset. Remember: your thoughts are not always facts. You can shape them to support your growth rather than hold you back.

Section 3: Stepping Out of Your Comfort Zone

Your "comfort zone" is the mental space where you feel safe and at ease because you're doing things you're used to. While staying in this zone might make you feel secure, it can limit your growth. True self-confidence often blooms when you challenge yourself—doing things that feel a bit scary or uncomfortable at first.

Why Leaving Your Comfort Zone Helps Confidence

1. **Discovering Hidden Abilities:** You might be better at certain tasks than you think. But you won't know unless you try.
2. **Learning Through Experience:** Even if you fail, you gain knowledge and skills. Over time, those lessons become the building blocks of confidence.
3. **Overcoming Fear:** Each time you do something you're afraid of, you prove to yourself that fear doesn't control you. This makes future challenges seem more manageable.

How to Push Your Boundaries Safely

- **Set Small, Specific Goals:** Don't jump straight to the hardest challenge. If you're scared of public speaking, start by talking in front of a small group of friends. Then, gradually increase the size of your audience.
- **Plan and Prepare:** If you know you're going to try something new—like traveling alone—do some research. Prepare what you need, whether that's reading a travel guide or practicing a skill. Being prepared reduces anxiety.
- **Visualize Success:** Before attempting the new activity, take a few moments to picture yourself doing it successfully. This can help your mind focus on a positive outcome.
- **Seek Support:** Ask a friend or mentor for advice, or invite someone to join you. Having support can reduce the fear factor and make the experience more fun.

Dealing with Discomfort

It's normal to feel awkward, scared, or anxious when you step out of your comfort zone. Rather than trying to make those feelings vanish, accept them as part of the growth process. A bit of discomfort shows you're learning something new. Over time, the activity that once felt scary becomes part of your comfort zone.

Celebrating Each Step

Whether your step is small—like speaking up in class—or large—like taking on a leadership role—recognize it. Give yourself credit for trying. Even if things don't go perfectly, you made progress by pushing your boundary. This positive reinforcement makes it easier to step out of your comfort zone again in the future.

Long-Term Benefits

When you regularly challenge yourself, you get used to adapting and learning. Your mindset shifts from "I'm afraid I'll fail" to "I can handle what comes next." This shift is the core of self-confidence: knowing you don't have to be perfect, just willing to try. Over time, you'll see that taking on new challenges becomes less intimidating and more exciting.

Stepping out of your comfort zone isn't always easy, but it's one of the most direct paths to greater self-confidence. Each new experience helps you realize that you're stronger, smarter, and more capable than you might have thought. And that realization fuels your next step forward.

Section 4: Building on Success and Embracing Mistakes

Confidence grows when you acknowledge your successes and learn from your mistakes. This balanced approach ensures that you give yourself enough credit for your achievements while also staying humble and open to growth.

Recognizing Success

1. **Track Your Achievements:** Write down your small and big successes in a journal. This could be anything from finishing a homework assignment on time to learning a new skill at work. Looking back through your list can boost your mood and show you how far you've come.
2. **Celebrate in Healthy Ways:** Reward yourself with something that makes you feel good—like sharing your win with a supportive friend, treating yourself to a favorite snack, or doing a small happy dance. Celebrations reinforce positive feelings and remind you that hard work pays off.
3. **Share with Others:** Telling a friend or family member about your progress can multiply the good feeling. Hearing them say "Well done!" can further boost your confidence. Just remember to also encourage their successes, so it feels like a two-way celebration.

Embracing Mistakes

On the flip side, mistakes and failures are unavoidable. They can be painful, but they also carry lessons:

1. **Accept Responsibility:** If something goes wrong, resisting the urge to blame others helps you learn more. Ask, "What could I have done differently?" or "What part of this did I control?"
2. **Identify the Lesson:** Each mistake offers insight. Maybe you learned that you need better time management, or perhaps you realized you should ask for help sooner. Extract that lesson and use it next time.
3. **Move On:** After analyzing a mistake, do your best to let it go. Dwelling on it for too long can damage your confidence. Instead, focus on how you'll improve in the future.
4. **Keep Perspective:** Making a mistake doesn't mean you are a failure. It simply means you tried something that didn't work out as planned. Even experts and professionals mess up sometimes.

The Balance Between Success and Failure

Life isn't all wins or losses; it's a mix. Overvaluing success can lead to perfectionism and burnout, while focusing too heavily on failure can cause discouragement. Recognizing both is key. Celebrate your achievements, learn from your errors, and stay motivated to keep growing.

Building a Growth Mindset

A "growth mindset" means believing you can improve your talents and intelligence with effort and practice. This mindset welcomes mistakes as part of learning. It also encourages you to keep pushing your limits. Self-confidence flourishes when you see yourself as a learner, not as someone who must get everything right on the first try.

Over time, a healthy relationship with success and failure makes you more resilient. You won't be overly crushed by a setback, nor will you rely solely on achievements for self-worth. You'll develop an inner confidence that stays steady, powered by the knowledge that every experience—good or bad—helps you move forward.

Section 5: Practical Habits to Strengthen Self-Confidence

Now that we've explored the mindset shifts that support self-confidence, let's look at some day-to-day habits you can develop. These actions may seem small, but done consistently, they can have a big impact on how you see yourself.

1. **Positive Morning Routine:** Start your day with something uplifting. This could be a short walk, a 5-minute meditation, or reading an inspirational quote. Setting a positive tone in the morning often carries through the rest of the day.
2. **Affirmations:** Repeating phrases like "I am capable," "I am worthy," or "I can learn anything I put my mind to" might feel strange at first, but it helps replace negative self-talk with kinder thoughts. Say them out loud or write them in a journal.
3. **Keep Learning:** Regularly pick up new skills or knowledge—like learning a language, playing an instrument, or trying a new craft. Each time you learn something new, you prove to yourself that you can grow.
4. **Dress in a Way That Makes You Feel Good:** You don't need expensive clothes to feel confident, but wearing clothes that fit well and reflect your style can boost self-esteem. It shows that you value yourself enough to present yourself comfortably and confidently.
5. **Posture Check:** Stand or sit up straight, with shoulders back and head held high. It might sound silly, but posture affects how you feel about yourself. Good posture often leads to feeling more self-assured.
6. **Practice Saying "No":** Part of confidence is respecting your own boundaries. If you feel overloaded, it's okay to say "no" to additional tasks or invitations. This doesn't make you selfish; it shows you understand your limits.
7. **Physical Activity:** Exercise doesn't just improve your body; it also releases endorphins that help you feel better mentally. Even a short daily walk or a quick home workout can give a sense of accomplishment.
8. **Reflect on Your Day:** Before bed, think of three things you did well, no matter how small. Maybe you helped a friend, or cleaned your

room, or tried a difficult math problem. This practice trains your mind to look for the positives.

Creating a Confidence-Building Environment

Try to surround yourself with people and influences that encourage you. This doesn't mean ignoring constructive feedback, but it does mean limiting negative or toxic voices that constantly bring you down. When possible, choose friends who uplift you, follow social media accounts that inspire you, and read books that enrich your mind.

Consistency Is Key

Small habits might seem powerless on their own, but over time, they build a stronger sense of who you are and what you can do. Each day, a little bit more practice, a little bit more courage, and a little bit more self-kindness will accumulate into something significant. That's how confidence blossoms: step by step, habit by habit, until you realize you're standing taller than before—proud of who you are and what you can achieve.

Chapter 12: Finding Motivation Every Day

Introduction

Motivation is the drive or desire that makes you want to take action. It's what gets you out of bed in the morning, pushes you to finish a project, or encourages you to practice a new skill. Without motivation, even simple tasks can feel like a chore. But with the right mindset, you can transform your daily routine into something more purposeful and engaging.

In this chapter, we'll explore how to find motivation and keep it going, even when you don't feel like doing anything. We'll discuss the different types of motivation—like being motivated by rewards or by passion—and how to use them to your advantage. We'll also look at common obstacles, such as feeling bored, overwhelmed, or discouraged, and what you can do to overcome them.

By the end of Chapter 12, you'll have a toolkit of ideas for jumpstarting your drive whenever it wanes. You'll learn how setting clear goals, finding meaning in your activities, and maintaining a positive environment can keep you energized and excited. Motivation doesn't always come naturally, but with practice and strategy, you can develop it as a daily habit that fuels your personal growth.

Section 1: Understanding Motivation

What Is Motivation?

Motivation is the internal or external force that makes you act toward a goal. It can come from inside you—like wanting to improve your health—or outside of you, like a reward or praise from others. Both types can be useful, but understanding how they work can help you stay driven more consistently.

Types of Motivation

1. **Intrinsic Motivation:** This is when you do something because you genuinely enjoy it or find it meaningful. For example, an artist who paints because they love expressing themselves is driven by intrinsic motivation. It tends to last longer because it's based on personal satisfaction.
2. **Extrinsic Motivation:** This is when you do something to earn a reward or avoid a punishment. For instance, studying hard to get good grades or to avoid parental disappointment. Extrinsic motivators can be helpful for tasks you're not naturally interested in, but they might not create long-lasting passion.

Why Motivation Fluctuates

1. **Lack of Clarity:** If you're not sure why you're doing something, you might lose interest. Clear goals often lead to better motivation.
2. **Burnout or Stress:** Pushing yourself too hard can drain your motivation over time. When you're exhausted, it's harder to feel excited about tasks.
3. **External Changes:** Life events—like moving to a new city or changing schools—can disrupt your usual routine. This can affect your motivation if you don't adapt your goals to the new situation.
4. **Negative Mindset:** Constant negative thinking or fear of failure can sap your motivation. If you believe you won't succeed, you're less likely to try your best.

The Link Between Motivation and Emotions

Your emotions play a huge role in motivation. When you feel happy or curious, you're more likely to jump into action. When you're sad or anxious, you might procrastinate or avoid tasks. Recognizing this link can help you make changes—like doing a mood-boosting activity (listening to music, going for a walk) before tackling your tasks.

Why Motivation Matters

Motivation propels you to learn new skills, overcome obstacles, and grow as a person. It helps you make progress in areas that are important to you, such as academics, sports, creative pursuits, or relationships. Without motivation, you might drift through life feeling unfulfilled or stuck. With it, you're more likely to push forward, adapt to challenges, and achieve goals that bring you happiness and success.

Understanding what motivation is—and what can influence it—sets the stage for using it effectively. In the next sections, we'll explore specific ways to boost your daily drive, even on days when you feel like staying under the covers. Motivation isn't a magic trick; it's a skill you can cultivate with knowledge, practice, and a supportive environment.

Section 2: Setting Clear and Meaningful Goals

Goals give your motivation direction. Without them, your energy can feel scattered or aimless. Setting clear and meaningful goals helps you focus on what truly matters to you.

The Power of a Good Goal

1. **Clarity:** A clear goal spells out exactly what you want to do. Instead of "I want to get better at math," say, "I want to improve my math grade from a C to a B by the end of the semester."
2. **Measurement:** When your goal is measurable, you know exactly when you've reached it. This helps you track progress and celebrate small wins.
3. **Challenge:** A goal that's too easy may not motivate you, and one that's too hard can lead to frustration. Find a balance—something that pushes you but feels achievable with effort.

Aligning Goals with Values

It's easier to stay motivated if your goals match your values or interests. For instance, if you deeply care about the environment, setting a goal to volunteer at a local cleanup or to reduce plastic use might energize you. If you love art, picking a goal that involves drawing or painting daily can spark intrinsic motivation.

Short-Term vs. Long-Term Goals

- **Short-Term Goals:** These might take days or weeks to complete—like finishing a book or saving up for a small purchase. They provide quick wins and keep you motivated on a regular basis.
- **Long-Term Goals:** These can take months or years—like learning a new language fluently or saving money for college. They give you a sense of direction in life. It's helpful to break them into smaller milestones.

Writing Down Your Goals

Putting goals on paper makes them feel more real. You can use a notebook, a planner, or even a digital app. List why the goal matters to you, the steps you plan to take, and a target date if applicable.

Reviewing and Revising Goals

Goals shouldn't be static. As you learn more about yourself or your situation changes, it's okay to adjust them. Maybe you discover a different area of math needs more work, or you realize you want to aim for a higher grade. A regular check-in—weekly or monthly—can help you see what's working or where you might need to try something new.

Celebrating Milestones

Don't wait until you reach the final goal to celebrate. Reward yourself for hitting key milestones or making steady progress. This keeps your motivation up and acknowledges the effort you've put in. Rewards can be simple: a break, a favorite treat, or sharing your progress with a supportive friend.

When your goals are well-defined, personally meaningful, and broken down into manageable steps, you give your motivation a clear path to follow. Goals act like a roadmap, helping you focus your energy and measure your successes along the way. With each milestone you achieve, your sense of motivation and self-belief grows stronger.

Section 3: Creating a Motivating Environment

Your surroundings can strongly influence your motivation—both the physical space you occupy and the people you interact with. By shaping your environment, you can set yourself up for success rather than constantly fighting distractions or negativity.

Organizing Your Physical Space

1. **Designated Work Areas:** If possible, have a specific spot for studying, working, or practicing a skill. Keep it tidy and stocked with the tools you need—like pens, notebooks, or your instrument. This helps your brain associate that spot with "time to get things done."
2. **Remove Distractions:** If your phone tempts you to scroll social media endlessly, keep it in another room or use a distraction-blocking app. The less you have to fight against interruptions, the easier it is to stay motivated.
3. **Personal Touches:** Decorate your workspace with motivational quotes, pictures of loved ones, or small objects that inspire you. These reminders can boost your mood and keep your goals in mind.

Choosing the Right People

1. **Positive Influences:** Spend more time with people who encourage your growth. This could be classmates who also care about doing well in school, coworkers who strive for excellence, or friends who share your hobbies and passions.
2. **Limit Negativity:** While you can't always avoid negative or discouraging people, you can minimize their impact. If someone constantly puts you down or distracts you from your goals, it may be best to keep some distance or set firm boundaries.
3. **Mentors and Role Models:** Finding someone who's achieved what you want can spark motivation. They don't have to be famous; a teacher, coach, or neighbor can be a powerful role model if they set a good example and offer guidance.

Digital Environment

1. **Curate Your Feeds:** Unfollow or mute accounts on social media that bring you down or cause endless distraction. Follow accounts that inspire you—like educational channels or positive communities.
2. **Use Technology Wisely:** Timers and productivity apps can help you stay on track. However, be careful not to let screens consume all your time. Balance online tools with real-world practice and interactions.

Healthy Routines

Create daily or weekly routines that support motivation:

- **Morning Routine:** Start each day with a simple practice—like writing down a key goal or doing a quick stretch.
- **Scheduled Breaks:** Plan short breaks to recharge, rather than working non-stop until you collapse.
- **Evening Review:** Spend a few minutes each night reflecting on what you did well and what you can improve tomorrow.

The Power of Environment

By deliberately shaping your environment—both physical and social—you make it easier to stay motivated. Instead of relying only on willpower, you set yourself up in a space and a community that naturally supports your goals. Over time, this supportive environment becomes a strong ally in your pursuit of a better, more driven version of yourself.

Section 4: Maintaining Motivation Through Challenges

Everyone faces days (or even longer periods) when motivation seems to disappear—maybe due to a difficult assignment, unexpected life changes, or emotional struggles. The key is learning how to cope with these challenges and keep going.

Recognizing the Warning Signs

1. **Feeling Overwhelmed:** You have a huge to-do list but feel unable to tackle it.
2. **Procrastination:** You continually delay tasks, avoiding them because they seem too hard or uninteresting.
3. **Loss of Interest:** You're suddenly bored by activities you once enjoyed.
4. **Negative Mood:** Stress, sadness, or frustration overshadow your usual excitement or drive.

Strategies to Reignite Motivation

1. **Break Down Overwhelming Tasks:** Large tasks can cause panic. Divide them into smaller parts. Completing the first small part can give you the boost needed to tackle the next.
2. **Adjust Your Plan:** Sometimes your original schedule or approach doesn't work anymore. Take a step back, see what went wrong, and try a different method.

3. **Seek Support:** Talk to a friend, teacher, or family member about your struggles. They might offer insights or simply lend a listening ear to help you feel less alone.
4. **Use Past Successes:** Remind yourself of times you overcame challenges. Thinking about a past victory can inspire you to believe you can succeed again.
5. **Incorporate Fun:** If you're studying, add elements of fun—like turning practice questions into a game, or rewarding yourself with something enjoyable after a focused work session.

Dealing with Discouragement

Sometimes, even your best efforts lead to slow progress or minor setbacks. How do you keep motivation alive then?

- **Accept the Struggle:** Remind yourself that struggling is part of learning. If it were easy, it wouldn't push you to grow.
- **Focus on Growth, Not Perfection:** Instead of measuring yourself against an impossible standard, measure your improvement from last week or last month. This shift in perspective can keep your spirits higher.
- **Acknowledge Feelings:** It's normal to feel disappointed or frustrated. Allow yourself to feel these emotions briefly, but don't let them define you. Then, refocus on your next step.

Building Resilience

Facing challenges can actually strengthen your motivation if you see them as lessons rather than roadblocks. Each time you confront a difficult situation and persevere, you prove to yourself that you can handle tough times. This builds a cycle of resilience:

1. **Challenge appears.**
2. **You struggle but keep trying.**
3. **You learn something new, even if the result isn't perfect.**
4. **You feel stronger and more capable.**

Over time, that cycle becomes a powerful force that fuels your motivation. You'll realize that obstacles aren't a sign to quit but an invitation to grow.

With each hurdle you overcome, you develop greater confidence in your ability to stay motivated, no matter what life throws at you.

Section 5: Everyday Practices to Boost Motivation

Having a toolkit of simple daily practices can help you maintain motivation. These small actions, when repeated consistently, can keep your energy and enthusiasm alive, even on tough days.

1. **Morning Mindset Check:** Soon after you wake up, spend a minute or two thinking about your main goal or focus for the day. Ask yourself, "What's one thing I can do today that will bring me closer to my goal?" This sets a purposeful tone.
2. **Habit Stacking:** Link a new habit to an existing habit. For instance, if you want to practice guitar daily, do it right after you finish dinner. This makes it easier to remember and keeps your motivation steady.
3. **Micro-Challenges:** Give yourself tiny challenges throughout the day. For example, "I'll focus on this homework for 10 minutes without checking my phone." These mini achievements can build into a bigger sense of accomplishment.
4. **Plan Breaks and Rewards:** Knowing that you have a break or small treat coming up can keep you motivated to work in focused bursts. Just ensure the break doesn't turn into a complete distraction—set a time limit.
5. **Reflect on Progress:** Each evening, note at least one thing you accomplished. It could be as simple as sending an important email or making progress on a reading assignment. Recognizing these successes, however small, fuels motivation for tomorrow.
6. **Gratitude Practice:** Spend a few moments thinking about three things you're grateful for. This can shift your perspective toward the positive and remind you why your efforts matter.
7. **Stay Inspired:** Watch motivational videos, listen to podcasts, or read about people who've achieved goals similar to yours. Hearing success stories can reignite your own ambition.

8. **Adjust as Needed:** If you find you're dreading a particular task every day, see if you can change the approach. Maybe do it at a different time or break it into smaller steps. Tweaking your routine can keep it fresh and less daunting.

Keeping It Realistic

Try not to cram too many practices into your day all at once. Start with one or two changes, then add more as they become routine. An overloaded schedule can hurt motivation rather than help it. The goal is to create an environment where motivation can thrive without becoming an extra source of stress.

Long-Term Impact

When you consistently follow these everyday practices, you'll likely see a positive shift in your overall mindset and energy levels. Tasks that once felt dull might become less of a chore. You'll also build confidence in your ability to control your motivation instead of waiting for inspiration to strike. Over the long run, these daily habits can make the difference between stumbling through life's demands and progressing toward the goals and dreams that matter most to you.

Chapter 13: Being Responsible for Your Life

Introduction

Responsibility is about taking charge of your actions, decisions, and the path your life follows. When you are responsible, you accept that the choices you make and the effort you put into things have real effects on your success and happiness. This mindset can be challenging at first, because it means you can't always blame others for your problems or wait for them to fix everything. However, once you understand and practice responsibility, you gain the power to shape your own destiny.

In this chapter, we will explore what it means to be responsible for your life. We will talk about accountability—admitting mistakes and learning from them. We will look at how every choice we make, big or small, influences our direction. We'll learn to stop making excuses and start focusing on finding solutions. You will see why blaming others might give you temporary relief, but ultimately holds you back from growth. We will also discuss how being responsible doesn't only affect you; it affects those around you, your community, and the world in small but meaningful ways.

By the end of this chapter, you will have practical tools to build a more responsible mindset. You will learn how to create your own path by making good decisions, caring for yourself, and respecting the people around you. Embracing responsibility can be life-changing: once you hold yourself accountable, you open the door to freedom, growth, and real control over your future.

Section 1: Understanding Responsibility

Responsibility can seem like a big word. Sometimes it might remind you of chores at home or rules at school. But responsibility is more than completing a list of tasks. At its core, responsibility means understanding that your actions and choices have consequences, and being willing to accept those consequences—good or bad—when they happen.

What Responsibility Really Means

1. **Owning Your Actions:** When you do something, you acknowledge that it was your decision. If it leads to a positive result, you celebrate. If it leads to a negative result, you learn from it.
2. **Recognizing Your Influence:** Even small actions can have a ripple effect. For example, if you help a classmate with homework, you brighten their day and maybe improve their score. If you spread gossip, you might harm someone's reputation. Taking responsibility means being aware that what you do can affect other people.
3. **Being Dependable:** Responsible people do their best to keep promises and show up on time. This helps others trust them. When people trust you, they respect you more and may give you more freedom or opportunities.

Responsibility vs. Obligation

You might wonder how responsibility differs from obligation. An obligation is something you must do—like paying taxes or attending school until a certain age. Responsibility is more about your mindset. You fulfill obligations because you have to, but you act responsibly because you choose to. A responsible student will not just show up in class but also put in effort to learn and be helpful, even if no one is telling them to do so.

Benefits of Embracing Responsibility

- **Personal Growth:** When you see that you have control over your actions, you naturally try to improve. You realize that studying harder leads to better grades, or that practicing a skill consistently leads to more mastery.
- **Reduced Blame:** If something goes wrong, you look inward first. Instead of blaming bad luck or other people, you ask, "What could I do better?" This attitude lets you fix issues faster.

- **Stronger Character:** Being responsible requires honesty, both with yourself and others. Over time, you become someone who is trustworthy, sincere, and respected.

Common Misunderstandings

Some people think responsibility means never asking for help. That's not true. In fact, a responsible person knows when they need assistance or guidance. They also recognize that responsibility doesn't mean always being right or being in control of everything. It's about doing your part and acknowledging the parts you can't control.

When you truly understand responsibility, you see it's not a burden but a chance to grow. You realize that your life is, to a large extent, shaped by your thoughts, choices, and behaviors. This realization can be empowering—it gives you the steering wheel of your own journey. You might still face difficult roads or unexpected turns, but you know that how you respond is ultimately in your hands.

Section 2: Accepting Accountability

Accountability is closely tied to responsibility. When you are accountable, you openly admit when you have made a mistake, failed to meet a promise, or hurt someone's feelings. Instead of hiding, denying, or blaming others, you step up and acknowledge your role. Although this can feel uncomfortable, it is a core part of growing into a mature and reliable individual.

Why Accountability Matters

1. **Honesty Builds Trust:** When you admit a mistake, people see you as honest. They realize you're not trying to shift blame or cover your tracks. Over time, this honesty strengthens relationships, whether with friends, teachers, or coworkers.
2. **Learning from Mistakes:** You can't learn from a mistake if you refuse to admit it happened. Accountability allows you to analyze

what went wrong and find ways to prevent the same mistake in the future.
3. **Personal Integrity:** Integrity means doing the right thing, especially when no one is watching. Being accountable to yourself—recognizing when you haven't met your own standards—strengthens your sense of integrity.

Challenges to Being Accountable

- **Fear of Punishment:** You might worry that admitting a mistake will lead to punishment or shame. While consequences are sometimes unavoidable, the long-term benefits of honesty usually outweigh the short-term discomfort.
- **Ego and Pride:** Sometimes you might think admitting an error makes you look weak. In reality, owning up shows strength of character. It proves you're confident enough to face the truth.
- **Unclear Boundaries:** If tasks and roles aren't clearly defined, it can be hard to know who's responsible for what. This can lead to confusion and finger-pointing.

Strategies for Embracing Accountability

1. **Reflect Before Responding:** When something goes wrong, pause before reacting. Ask yourself what role you played. Even if you weren't entirely at fault, acknowledge your part.
2. **Apologize Sincerely:** If your actions harmed someone, offer a genuine apology. Explain what you will do differently next time. Empty apologies that sound forced don't rebuild trust.
3. **Make It Right:** If possible, fix the mistake. That might mean redoing a task, replacing something broken, or having a heartfelt talk to mend a relationship. Taking steps to correct the issue shows you're truly committed to accountability.
4. **Learn and Move On:** Accountability doesn't mean dwelling on guilt forever. Once you've owned up and tried to fix the situation, let yourself move forward. Apply the lessons learned to avoid repeat errors.

The Ripple Effect of Accountability

When you model accountability, you encourage others to do the same. This can create a healthier environment, be it at home, in school, or at work, where everyone takes ownership of their responsibilities. Blame games become less common, and people become more focused on solutions rather than excuses.

In short, accepting accountability might be tough, but it's a powerful way to become a more responsible and trustworthy person. It clears the path for better problem-solving, stronger relationships, and meaningful personal growth.

Section 3: The Power of Choices

Every day, you make countless choices—some small (like what to eat for breakfast) and some big (like which school club to join). You may not realize it, but these choices add up to form your habits, character, and future opportunities. Recognizing the power of choice is a crucial step toward being responsible for your life.

Why Choices Matter

1. **They Shape Your Path:** One decision can lead to another. For example, choosing to spend time studying math every day might help you get into a better college, which then affects your entire career path.
2. **They Reflect Your Values:** The choices you make—like volunteering in the community or helping a sibling—tell others what you care about. Over time, these actions build your reputation.
3. **They Build or Break Habits:** If you repeatedly choose to procrastinate, you create a habit of putting things off. If you consistently choose to go for a run in the morning, you form a habit that improves your health.

Overcoming Decision Fatigue

Sometimes, having too many choices can feel overwhelming, a phenomenon known as "decision fatigue." You may get tired of making decisions and start picking random or easy options just to get it over with. To manage this:

- **Plan Routine Decisions:** Decide on things like when to wake up, what to eat for breakfast, or what clothes to wear in advance. This saves mental energy for bigger decisions.
- **Set Clear Priorities:** Knowing what's most important helps you quickly sort your choices. If health is a priority, you might choose a healthy snack instead of junk food.
- **Limit Options:** If you find yourself lost in too many possibilities, narrow them down to two or three. This makes it easier to compare and decide.

Owning Your Choices

Responsibility for your life means standing behind your decisions. Sometimes you will choose well, sometimes poorly. Owning your choices involves:

1. **Thinking Before Acting:** Weigh the pros and cons, consider the potential outcomes, and reflect on whether the choice aligns with your goals or values.
2. **Accepting the Results:** If a choice leads to success, celebrate! If it leads to a setback, learn the lesson. The important part is acknowledging your role in it.
3. **Seeking Guidance (When Needed):** It's wise to ask for advice if you're unsure. Talking to parents, teachers, or friends can provide new viewpoints. However, the final decision still rests on you.

The Freedom in Choosing

Some people feel that having to make so many choices is stressful. But it can also be liberating once you realize you are not just a passenger in life. You get to steer. That freedom can inspire you to consider your values more deeply and act in a way that brings out your best self.

Embracing the power of your choices can lead to a life guided by purpose rather than random chance. Over time, this will help you build confidence in your decision-making abilities and deepen your sense of responsibility for your own path.

Section 4: Building Self-Reliance

Self-reliance means trusting in your own abilities to handle tasks, solve problems, and meet your needs. A self-reliant person understands that while help from others can be valuable, depending too much on external help can prevent growth. Being self-reliant is part of taking responsibility for your life because it involves learning to solve challenges on your own whenever possible.

Why Self-Reliance Is Important

1. **Greater Independence:** When you can fix a computer glitch yourself or cook your own meals, you rely less on others. This independence can boost your confidence and sense of freedom.
2. **Stronger Problem-Solving Skills:** Figuring out solutions on your own often involves creativity and research. Each problem you solve alone builds your ability to face bigger challenges.
3. **Better Resilience:** Life is full of surprises—illness, financial troubles, school changes. A self-reliant mindset helps you adapt because you trust you can handle unexpected obstacles.

Balancing Help and Self-Reliance

Self-reliance doesn't mean rejecting all assistance. Wise people know the difference between tasks they can do by themselves and situations where they might need guidance. Perhaps you can easily figure out how to fix a broken bike chain, but you need a mentor to understand advanced calculus. The key is to try on your own first, and then seek help when it's truly necessary.

Practical Ways to Build Self-Reliance

1. **Learn Basic Life Skills:** Skills like cooking, budgeting money, or doing laundry may seem small, but they add up to greater independence.
2. **Practice Critical Thinking:** Before asking someone to fix a problem, try to brainstorm solutions. Even if your ideas aren't perfect, you're training your mind to solve issues.
3. **Set Personal Goals:** Self-improvement targets—like learning to play the guitar or mastering a foreign language—encourage you to rely on your own discipline and determination.
4. **Take Calculated Risks:** Sometimes, you won't know if you can do something until you try. Push yourself to attempt tasks that feel slightly outside your comfort zone. Each success makes you more self-reliant.

Mindset Shift: "I Can Figure It Out"

One mental trick is to repeat phrases like, "I can figure it out," or "I can find a way." This doesn't mean you'll never fail. It means you believe your effort can lead to progress. When you start from the assumption that solutions exist, you train your brain to look for possibilities rather than obstacles.

The Impact on Responsibility

Being self-reliant is a big part of being responsible because it teaches you that your life outcomes often depend on what you do. If you rely too much on others, you might blame them when things go wrong. But if you know you can do a lot on your own, you're more inclined to take ownership of your actions and keep improving. This spirit of independence blends with accountability to form a mature, responsible approach to life.

Section 5: Overcoming Excuses and Blame

It's easy to blame traffic for making you late, your teacher for giving "unfair" tests, or your siblings for distracting you from your homework. While external factors do matter, constantly using them as excuses can stop you from being responsible and growing. Being responsible means recognizing that—no matter the situation—you still have some control over how you react and what you do next.

Why People Make Excuses

1. **Fear of Failure:** Admitting you fell short can feel scary. Excuses provide a temporary shield to protect your self-esteem.
2. **Laziness or Avoidance:** Sometimes, people make excuses to avoid extra work or the discomfort of trying something difficult.
3. **Habit:** If you grew up seeing people around you blaming others, you might learn to do the same without realizing it.

The Downside of Blame

- **Stuck Mindset:** When you blame other factors, you don't learn from your own mistakes. You miss the chance to adjust and do better next time.
- **Damaged Relationships:** Constantly blaming others can cause tension with friends or family. They might feel unfairly targeted or grow tired of hearing the same complaints.
- **Loss of Control:** If you always point fingers outward, you hand over your power. You're essentially saying that someone else or something else determines your success, leaving you feeling powerless.

Moving Past Excuses

1. **Identify Patterns:** Notice when you tend to blame or make excuses. Is it about being late, missing deadlines, or not performing well? Identifying where you slip helps you focus on those areas.
2. **Ask "What Can I Do?":** Shift your mindset from complaining to problem-solving. Even if the bus was late, could you have left earlier? If a teacher's test style is tough, could you change your study methods or ask for help?

3. **Set Realistic Expectations:** Sometimes, we make excuses because our goals are too big or unrealistic. Adjust your expectations and plan to achieve them step by step.
4. **Practice Self-Honesty:** Own up to your part in any situation. If you truly did everything you could, then accept that some things are beyond your control. If you find you didn't do enough, be honest and make a plan to do better next time.

The Mental Switch

Adopting a "no excuses" outlook doesn't mean ignoring genuine obstacles. It means focusing on what you can control rather than what you can't. For instance, if you're in a noisy environment, you might use noise-canceling headphones to study. You can't change the noise outside, but you can change your response to it.

Gaining Strength Through Responsibility

Dropping excuses and blame is liberating. It might feel uncomfortable initially, but it allows you to see where you can improve. This approach fosters growth, maturity, and a stronger sense of independence. You start realizing that your choices shape your life, and you become more motivated to make better ones.

Section 6: Developing a Solution-Focused Mindset

A solution-focused mindset is one where you look at a problem and immediately start thinking, "How can I fix this or make it better?" rather than "This is too hard," or "I can't do anything about it." Adopting this perspective is a key step in being responsible for your life because it drives you to take action instead of waiting for someone else to solve your problems.

Why Focus on Solutions?

1. **Reduces Worry:** When you dwell on a problem, your mind gets stuck in loops of negative thinking. Shifting to solutions interrupts that cycle and helps you use your energy productively.
2. **Boosts Confidence:** Each time you find a solution—no matter how small—you prove to yourself that you can handle challenges. This builds self-trust and encourages you to tackle bigger issues in the future.
3. **Sparks Creativity:** Problem-solving often involves thinking outside the box. The more you practice, the better you get at creative thinking, which is valuable in all areas of life—from academics to hobbies to relationships.

Steps to Foster a Solution-Focused Mindset

1. **Define the Problem Clearly:** Identify what the real issue is. For example, if you're doing poorly in math, is the issue your study method, lack of practice, or misunderstanding key concepts?
2. **Brainstorm Options:** Come up with multiple ways to address the problem, no matter how small or big the ideas seem. Write them down. The aim is to have a variety of potential solutions.
3. **Evaluate Pros and Cons:** Look at each idea and consider its advantages, possible drawbacks, and resources needed. This helps you pick the most practical option to try first.
4. **Take Action Quickly:** Don't wait too long to test a solution. If it works, great! If not, learn from it and try another. Speedy action prevents you from overthinking and losing motivation.
5. **Reflect and Adjust:** After trying a solution, ask yourself what worked and what didn't. Use that information to refine your approach. This continuous improvement cycle helps you solve bigger problems over time.

Attitude Shifts

- **Replace "I Can't" with "I'll Try."** Words influence your mindset. Committing to try opens the door to unexpected solutions.

- **View Failures as Experiments:** Not all solutions will succeed. Treat each attempt like an experiment: if it fails, you have data about what doesn't work.
- **Celebrate Small Wins:** When you do find a partial fix or slight improvement, acknowledge it. This momentum fuels further problem-solving efforts.

Benefits Beyond Problem-Solving

A solution-focused approach doesn't just help you with immediate issues. It reshapes how you see challenges in general, boosting resilience and responsibility. Instead of feeling helpless in the face of difficulties, you'll feel empowered to brainstorm ideas, ask for help if needed, and implement solutions. This proactive stance becomes a lifelong skill, beneficial in careers, relationships, and personal goals. Essentially, it keeps you in the driver's seat of your life.

Section 7: Extending Responsibility to Others and Community

Responsibility isn't only about taking care of your personal life. It also involves how you contribute to the well-being of people around you—family, friends, neighbors, and even strangers in your community. Being responsible for your life includes acknowledging the role you play in society and acting in ways that make life better for all.

Community Responsibility

1. **Volunteering:** Giving your time to community projects, local charities, or even neighborhood cleanups is a direct way to be responsible beyond yourself. This not only helps others but can also improve your sense of purpose.
2. **Kindness and Politeness:** Simple acts like opening a door for someone, returning a lost item, or offering to help a classmate with

homework spread positivity. These small gestures show you understand your influence on others.
3. **Environmental Care:** Taking responsibility for your environment—like recycling, reducing waste, or conserving water—helps preserve resources for future generations. Your daily choices, such as carrying a reusable water bottle instead of buying plastic bottles, matter more than you might think.

Helping Others vs. Doing Everything

While it's kind to help, remember that being responsible doesn't mean you have to solve everyone else's problems. There's a balance:

- **Encourage Self-Reliance:** You can guide someone to find their own solutions rather than doing everything for them. This is especially true in group projects, where each person needs to carry their part.
- **Avoid Burnout:** Overcommitting to help everyone, all the time, can lead to stress. Know your limits and practice self-care so you can continue being helpful in the long run.

Being a Role Model

When you demonstrate responsibility—arriving on time, doing your share of group tasks, admitting mistakes—others notice. If you're in a leadership position (like a team captain or a club officer), your actions can set a tone for the whole group. People often follow by example more than by instructions.

Community-Oriented Mindset

- **Active Citizenship:** If you're old enough, voting or participating in local meetings can shape your community's direction. Even if you're not of voting age, speaking up about issues or joining youth councils can make a difference.
- **Respect Public Spaces:** Public parks, libraries, and roads are shared resources. Treating them with care—throwing away trash, following rules—shows respect for everyone's well-being.

- **Online Conduct:** Responsibility extends to social media interactions, too. Posting respectful comments and avoiding cyberbullying contribute to a healthier online community.

Mutual Benefit

Engaging in community responsibility can seem like extra work. However, the benefits circle back. A cleaner neighborhood is nicer to live in, supportive neighbors may return the favor when you're in need, and a respectful online environment makes digital spaces more positive for everyone—including you.

When you broaden your view of responsibility from "just me" to "us," you enrich your life and the lives of others. You not only handle your personal duties but also help create a supportive, thriving environment. This expanded sense of responsibility is a hallmark of true maturity, reflecting compassion and wisdom in how you relate to the world.

Chapter 14: Embracing Gratitude and Kindness

Introduction

Gratitude and kindness are two qualities that can turn ordinary moments into joyful experiences. When you practice gratitude, you focus on the good things you have—like your health, supportive friends, or simple comforts. This mindset helps you appreciate life more. Kindness, on the other hand, is the act of showing care, empathy, and helpfulness toward others. By giving kindness, you create positive energy not just for the people you help, but also for yourself.

In this chapter, we'll explore why gratitude and kindness are so powerful. We'll talk about how being thankful can change your perspective, making you happier and more resilient. We'll see that kindness isn't just about big gestures—like donating large sums of money—but also about daily small acts, like giving compliments or lending a hand. We'll go through practical tips for building these habits into your everyday life and discuss common obstacles, such as feeling too busy or fearing rejection.

By the end, you'll have strategies to make gratitude and kindness a natural part of who you are. Embracing these qualities can improve your relationships, boost your mental well-being, and even enhance your physical health. Life feels more meaningful when you notice and appreciate the good, and actively share goodness with others. Let's discover how this approach can transform your day-to-day experiences.

Section 1: Understanding Gratitude

What Is Gratitude?

Gratitude means recognizing and appreciating the positive aspects of your life, even if things aren't perfect. It's not about ignoring problems or pretending everything is wonderful. Instead, it's about noticing the good—like a safe home, a friend who checks on you, or even your pet's silly antics—and feeling thankful.

Why Gratitude Matters

1. **Improved Mood:** When you focus on what you're thankful for, your brain releases chemicals that help you feel happier. You become less likely to dwell on worries.
2. **Better Relationships:** Expressing gratitude shows people you value them. They feel appreciated, which can strengthen your bond.
3. **Resilience:** In tough times, gratitude can shift your perspective. While you acknowledge the difficulty, you also remember that you still have resources or supportive people in your life.

Gratitude vs. Complacency

Some people worry that being grateful means settling for less. That's a misunderstanding. You can be thankful for what you have and still strive for more. Gratitude simply helps you avoid constant dissatisfaction. You can simultaneously acknowledge blessings and work toward goals.

Building a Gratitude Practice

- **Keep a Gratitude Journal:** Write down three things you're thankful for each day. They can be as simple as "a tasty breakfast" or "a friend who made me laugh."
- **Share Gratitude with Others:** If someone did something kind for you, tell them how much it meant. A simple "Thank you, I really appreciate this" can brighten their day.
- **Mindful Moments:** Pause before meals or at bedtime to reflect on good events or small pleasures, like a cozy blanket or a bright sunset.

Overcoming Obstacles to Gratitude

- **Busy Schedules:** If you're always rushing, you might forget to notice good things. Setting a daily reminder on your phone or scheduling a minute of gratitude can help.
- **Negative Environments:** If people around you complain a lot, it can rub off on you. Try to balance it with your own gratitude practice or share positive observations with them.
- **Comparison:** Constantly comparing your life to others' can make you feel less grateful. Remember, social media often shows only highlights. Focus on your own journey.

Long-Term Benefits

Regularly practicing gratitude can lead to:

- **Lower Stress Levels:** Grateful thoughts can interrupt stress cycles.
- **Improved Self-Esteem:** You feel better about yourself when you recognize the positives in your life.
- **More Positive Outlook:** Over time, you'll train your brain to spot good things automatically, rather than just focusing on problems.

Gratitude acts like a lens that brings your blessings into clearer view. By choosing to look through this lens each day, you shift from a mindset of "not enough" to one of thankfulness for what you already have. This doesn't mean ignoring life's challenges, but it does mean you carry a sense of appreciation that can guide you through them.

Section 2: The Power of Kindness

Defining Kindness

Kindness involves caring about other people's well-being and taking action to support or comfort them. It can be as easy as smiling at a neighbor, offering a helping hand, or sending an encouraging text to a friend. Even small acts of kindness add up, creating a ripple effect that can brighten communities and foster stronger connections.

Why Kindness Matters

1. **Fosters Connection:** When you're kind, you show that you acknowledge another person's value. This can break barriers between strangers, making it easier to start conversations or form friendships.
2. **Boosts Your Mood:** Research suggests that doing kind deeds releases feel-good hormones like oxytocin. People who help others often experience a "helper's high," a warm feeling of satisfaction.
3. **Counteracts Negativity:** In a world that can sometimes feel harsh—filled with competition or anger—kindness stands out. It offers hope and positivity, reminding everyone that compassion still exists.

Types of Kindness

- **Spontaneous Acts:** Holding a door open, letting someone merge in traffic, picking up a pen someone dropped. These small gestures show awareness and respect.
- **Planned Acts:** Volunteering at a local shelter, organizing a fundraising event, or participating in community drives. These require more time but can have a big impact.
- **Emotional Support:** Listening to someone who's upset, offering comforting words, or simply being present so they feel less alone.

Overcoming Barriers to Kindness

- **Shyness or Fear:** You might worry about how people will react. But most people appreciate thoughtfulness, even if they're surprised. Start small—like offering a genuine compliment.
- **Busy Lifestyles:** You may feel you have no time to help. However, kindness doesn't always require major efforts. Even a few seconds to say "You've done a great job" can matter.
- **Negative Experiences:** Maybe you tried being kind to someone who responded rudely. While hurtful, it doesn't negate the value of

kindness. Each act of kindness is still important, and many people will respond positively.

Linking Kindness to Responsibility

When you're responsible for your life, you also understand how your actions affect others. Kindness is a form of responsibility toward your community. You accept that you play a part in the emotional climate around you. Whether that climate is supportive or hostile depends, in some measure, on how you treat people day to day.

The Shared Benefits

Interestingly, kindness often benefits the giver as much as—or sometimes more than—the receiver. When you do something nice for someone else, you reinforce the belief that you can make a difference. This strengthens your self-esteem and sense of purpose. It also creates a cycle of positivity: your kindness might inspire another act of kindness, and so on.

In a nutshell, kindness turns empathy and compassion into action. It's a simple yet powerful way to connect with others, improve your mood, and make a meaningful contribution to the world. Even if your act seems small, remember it might be huge to the person on the receiving end.

Section 3: Connecting Gratitude and Kindness

Gratitude and kindness often go hand in hand. When you feel grateful, you're more inclined to spread goodwill. And when you practice kindness, you often find new things to be thankful for, such as the joy of helping someone in need.

How Gratitude Fuels Kindness

1. **Appreciation of Shared Humanity:** Recognizing how others have helped you can make you want to help them back or help others in

a similar position. For instance, if a teacher took extra time to tutor you, you might volunteer to tutor a younger student.
2. **Positive Emotions:** Gratitude lifts your mood. A good mood makes you more open to performing kind acts, whether it's sending a heartfelt message or volunteering for a community event.
3. **Deeper Sense of Abundance:** When you focus on the blessings in your life, you notice you have enough—sometimes more than enough—to share. This realization can drive you to give resources, time, or attention to those who lack them.

How Kindness Sparks Gratitude

1. **Appreciation from Others:** When people receive your kindness, they often express gratitude. Their "thank you" or smile can make you realize how fortunate you are to be in a position to help.
2. **New Friendships and Experiences:** Acts of kindness can lead to unexpected friendships or experiences. Later, you feel grateful for these new connections.
3. **Self-Esteem Boost:** Knowing you made a positive impact can make you thankful for your own abilities, resources, and the chance to make a difference.

Creating a Gratitude-Kindness Cycle

- **Reflect on Who Has Helped You:** Maybe a friend gave you moral support during a tough time. Think about ways you could "pay it forward," such as cheering up another friend or even a stranger.
- **Keep a Dual Journal:** Alongside listing what you're grateful for, list daily acts of kindness—either ones you performed or received. This fosters a heightened awareness of both.
- **Link Kindness to Gratitude Routines:** If you have a family dinner tradition of sharing something you're grateful for, include a question like, "How did you show kindness today?" This discussion can encourage everyone to do more good deeds.

Uplifting Communities

When gratitude and kindness become normal, entire communities can change. People become more supportive, less critical. This doesn't mean problems disappear, but challenges can be met with shared effort and goodwill. Over time, a simple "thank you" or helpful gesture can grow into a stronger sense of unity.

Combining gratitude with kindness is a powerful way to multiply positive feelings in your life. Each feeds off the other: your appreciation of blessings leads you to spread kindness, and acts of kindness generate even more reasons for gratitude. This cycle enriches not only your life but also the lives of those you touch.

Section 4: Practical Ways to Practice Gratitude Daily

Gratitude isn't just a concept; it's a habit you can develop through consistent practice. By integrating small routines into your day, you can make gratitude a natural part of your life.

1. Morning Gratitude Statements

Right after you wake up, think of one or two things you're grateful for. It could be as simple as "I'm thankful for a restful night's sleep," or "I'm grateful for the sunny weather today." This brief practice sets a positive tone for the hours ahead.

2. Gratitude Journaling

Keeping a journal is one of the most popular gratitude practices. Spend five minutes each night writing down things you appreciated that day. They might be:

- Big events, like a friend's birthday party.

- Small joys, like finding a funny video or trying a tasty new snack.
- Personal achievements, like completing a hard exercise routine.

Over time, flipping through your journal can remind you of the positive moments you might otherwise forget.

3. Gratitude Reminders

- **Digital Alerts:** Set an alarm on your phone once or twice a day to pause and name something you're grateful for.
- **Sticky Notes:** Place short gratitude messages on your mirror, desk, or computer.
- **Gratitude Apps:** Some apps prompt you to record daily thanks, offering motivational quotes or progress trackers.

4. Gratitude Conversations

Instead of complaining about your day, challenge yourself to share a highlight or positive aspect with a friend or family member. For example, during dinner, you could say, "I'm really thankful for how my coworker helped me today," or ask, "What was the best part of your day?" This small shift can create a more uplifting atmosphere.

5. Thank-You Notes

Writing thank-you notes to people who have impacted you—teachers, friends, family members—can deeply strengthen those bonds. It could be a simple text message or a handwritten letter. The act of composing your thoughts and putting them on paper helps you realize the depth of your gratitude.

6. Mindful Observations

Whenever you step outside, take a few seconds to appreciate something around you. Maybe it's the color of the sky, the shape of the clouds, or the sound of birds chirping. Recognizing everyday beauty can train your mind to notice positive details you used to overlook.

7. Combining Gratitude with Other Routines

Try pairing gratitude with other habits:

- **Before meals:** Pause briefly to appreciate the food.
- **During exercise:** Thank your body for what it can do.
- **Before sleep:** Reflect on the day's positive moments, giving you a calmer mind for rest.

Progress, Not Perfection

You don't have to become a perfect beacon of gratitude overnight. Some days, you'll forget or struggle to find things to appreciate, especially if you're stressed or upset. That's okay. The goal is to build a consistent pattern of noticing the good. Over time, you'll find it easier and more natural to express thanks, and your life will feel richer because of it.

Section 5: Incorporating Kindness Into Everyday Life

Acts of kindness can be woven into almost any moment of your daily life. You don't need to wait for a special occasion or a major crisis to help someone. Often, the simplest acts—done quietly—have the greatest impact.

1. Start with Small Gestures

- **Hold the Door:** This common courtesy can make someone's day a bit smoother.
- **Offer Genuine Compliments:** Instead of just saying "Nice job," be specific: "I really admired how you handled that question in class" or "I love your creativity on this project."
- **Pick Up Litter:** If you see trash lying around, take the initiative to throw it away. It's a small step toward a cleaner environment.

2. Schedule "Kindness Time"

Just as you schedule work or exercise, consider setting aside 10-15 minutes for a kindness activity. This could be checking in on a lonely neighbor, sending an encouraging message to a friend, or helping a sibling with homework. When kindness is part of your routine, it becomes second nature.

3. Offer Help, Not Criticism

If you spot someone struggling—like a classmate confused by a math problem—ask if they'd like help. Even if you can't fix the entire problem, your willingness to assist can lift their spirits. Approach them in a gentle way that says, "I'm here if you need me," rather than, "You're doing it wrong."

4. Practicing Empathy

Kindness grows stronger when combined with empathy—the ability to sense or understand someone else's feelings. Listening to a friend who is going through a hard time, validating their concerns, or just being present can be an act of tremendous kindness. Empathy drives you to respond in caring, thoughtful ways that go beyond a quick gesture.

5. Give Second Chances

Sometimes, showing kindness means letting go of grudges or resentments. If a friend apologized for a mistake, consider forgiving them. Carrying anger often hurts you more than the other person. Forgiveness can pave the way for healing and stronger bonds.

6. Community and Global Kindness

- **Volunteer:** Hospitals, animal shelters, libraries, and community centers often need volunteers. Offering even a few hours a week can make a huge difference.
- **Donate or Share Resources:** If you have items you no longer use, donate them to charities or local families who might need them.

You can also share knowledge, like teaching someone a skill or language.
- **Social Media Positivity:** Instead of leaving negative comments online, spread kindness through uplifting messages or constructive feedback. Simple acts like praising someone's artwork or sharing an inspirational quote can foster a kinder digital environment.

7. Recognize Your Limits

Being kind doesn't mean you let people take advantage of you. Healthy boundaries are important. You can show compassion while also respecting your own time and energy. Kindness is most powerful when it's given freely, not forced out of guilt or obligation.

Kindness is like a muscle: the more you use it, the stronger it becomes. Each day, you have countless opportunities to brighten someone's mood, offer a helping hand, or spread positivity. Over time, you'll see how these everyday acts, small as they may be, create a more caring, supportive world—and help you become a more open-hearted and fulfilled individual.

Chapter 15: Communicating Clearly and Respectfully

Introduction

Communication is a core skill that affects almost every part of life. Whether you're talking with friends, family, teachers, co-workers, or even strangers, the way you communicate can determine how well you understand each other, how conflicts get resolved, and how close your relationships become. In many ways, your personal and professional success depends on how well you can express your thoughts and listen to others.

In this chapter, we will explore **communicating clearly and respectfully**, covering both verbal and nonverbal elements. We'll talk about speaking with honesty and clarity, plus the importance of listening with genuine interest. We will dive into how tone, body language, and choice of words matter. We'll also look at digital communication, such as texting and social media, because in today's world, much of our interaction happens online. Effective communication is not only about choosing the right words but also about maintaining respect for others' viewpoints—even when you disagree.

By the end, you'll have practical tools for giving and receiving feedback, resolving conflicts without insults or shouting, and building stronger connections. You'll learn that real communication isn't just about talking; it's about creating a safe environment where everyone feels heard and valued. This skill forms the backbone of healthy friendships, family ties, work relationships, and even casual encounters. Let's discover how we can speak and listen in ways that respect both ourselves and those around us, fostering mutual understanding and more positive interactions overall.

Section 1: The Foundations of Clear Communication

Clear communication begins with understanding what you want to say and why. If you lack clarity in your own mind, your words can become confusing or muddled for the person hearing them. It may lead to misunderstandings, wasted effort, or even conflict. Here are some core elements to keep in mind:

1. **Know Your Purpose:** Before starting a conversation, think: "What am I hoping to achieve?" Are you giving instructions, sharing a feeling, or asking for help? Being clear on your own goal helps shape the words you choose.
2. **Organize Your Thoughts:** If you're about to explain something complex, consider outlining key points mentally or jotting them down. This ensures you don't leave out important information or wander off-topic.
3. **Use Plain Language:** Complex words or jargon can make you sound impressive, but they can also confuse people. Whenever possible, use simple, direct words that convey your meaning precisely. For instance, instead of saying, "I am endeavoring to elucidate the intricacies," say, "I want to clarify the details." Clarity, not complexity, should be your priority.
4. **Be Specific and Concrete:** Vague statements like "You never help me" or "That's really interesting" can be interpreted in many ways. Instead, be specific: "Could you help me clean the garage this Saturday?" or "I find the way you solved that math problem interesting because you used a different formula."
5. **Mind Your Pace:** Some people talk very fast, others talk slowly. Being conscious of your pace helps listeners absorb your information. Speak fast enough to hold interest, yet slow enough that people can process what you're saying. Pause after key points so the listener has time to think.
6. **Check for Understanding:** After explaining a concept or giving instructions, you might ask, "Does that make sense?" or "Would you like me to clarify anything?" This gentle check ensures the other person truly grasps your message rather than just nodding politely.

7. **Consider Your Listener's Perspective:** Effective communicators tailor their message to their audience. If you're talking to a child, you might use simpler language and more examples. If you're speaking with a professional colleague, you might use technical terms but still ensure clarity.

When you establish these foundational habits—knowing your purpose, organizing your thoughts, and speaking in straightforward language—your words become more transparent to others. You reduce the risk of confusion and pave the way for more meaningful conversations. Over time, these small improvements in clarity can have a big impact on the success of your personal and professional interactions.

Section 2: Respect in Communication—Tone, Word Choice, and Body Language

Clarity is essential, but so is respect. The way you say something can be just as impactful as what you say. Respectful communication fosters trust, prevents misunderstandings from escalating, and helps maintain healthy relationships.

Tone

1. **Speak Calmly:** Even if you disagree strongly, yelling or speaking in a sarcastic tone usually shuts down real dialogue. A calm, measured voice encourages others to stay open to what you're saying.
2. **Avoid Mockery:** Ridiculing or taunting someone—either openly or subtly—makes them defensive. This quickly derails any chance of cooperation or understanding.
3. **Use a Polite Manner:** Words like "please," "thank you," and "excuse me" might seem old-fashioned, but they signal courtesy and respect. Small politeness markers can make a big difference in how your message is received.

Word Choice

1. **Positive or Neutral Phrasing**: Instead of saying "You're always wrong," try "I see it differently" or "I have a different opinion." Softening your language can preserve goodwill.
2. **First-Person Statements**: Using "I" statements can reduce the sense of blame. For example, say "I feel upset when this happens" rather than "You make me so angry."
3. **Avoid Absolutes**: Words like "always" and "never" are rarely true. Saying "You always forget to text me back" can make the other person feel attacked, whereas "Sometimes I don't hear from you, and it worries me" is more accurate and less accusatory.

Body Language

1. **Maintain Appropriate Eye Contact:** Looking someone in the eye shows sincerity and attention. Avoiding eye contact might signal nervousness or dishonesty, while staring too intensely can appear aggressive. Strike a comfortable balance.
2. **Open Posture:** Crossing your arms or turning your body away might suggest you're closed off or disinterested. Keep your posture relaxed but attentive—face the other person and keep your shoulders down and back.
3. **Nodding and Smiling (When Appropriate):** Subtle nods and occasional smiles can show you're engaged and understanding. Be genuine—fake smiles or over-exaggerated nods can look insincere.
4. **Watch Your Hands and Feet:** Fidgeting, tapping your foot, or constantly checking your phone can distract or offend the person speaking. Show you're present and interested by keeping these habits in check.

Balancing Assertiveness and Respect

Being respectful doesn't mean letting others walk all over you. You can be firm about your needs or boundaries while still communicating kindly. For instance, if someone keeps interrupting, you can say, "I'd like to finish my point, please," instead of snapping, "Stop talking over me!" Assertiveness plus respect fosters more productive conversations.

When you pay attention to tone, word choice, and body language, you create an atmosphere where people feel safe to express themselves. You demonstrate empathy, which can encourage mutual respect. As a result, disagreements become easier to handle, and everyday interactions feel more positive and collaborative.

Section 3: The Art of Listening Actively

Communication is not just about talking; it's equally about **listening**. Active listening involves giving someone your full attention, seeking to understand their viewpoint, and responding thoughtfully. This skill can dramatically improve your relationships because it shows that you respect and value what the other person has to say.

Key Components of Active Listening

1. **Full Attention:** Set aside distractions. Put down your phone, pause the TV, or step away from the computer. Face the speaker and make eye contact. Show with your body language that you're fully present.
2. **Minimal Interruptions:** Let the speaker finish their thoughts before jumping in. Constantly cutting someone off can break their flow and discourage them from sharing more.
3. **Reflect and Clarify:** After the person speaks, summarize what you heard: "So you're saying you're stressed because the deadline got moved up?" This helps you confirm your understanding and shows you've been paying attention.
4. **Ask Open-Ended Questions:** Instead of just "Did you like it?" try "What did you think about the experience?" Open-ended questions invite the speaker to elaborate, giving you deeper insight into their feelings or ideas.

Benefits of Active Listening

1. **Reduced Misunderstandings:** When people feel truly heard, they're more likely to clarify their points if you missed something. This prevents confusion from escalating into conflict.
2. **Stronger Bonds:** Listening actively sends a message that you care. This fosters trust and can bring you closer to friends, family, or colleagues.
3. **Better Problem-Solving:** In group settings, truly hearing everyone's perspective often leads to more creative solutions. If each voice is heard, the final decision can be stronger and more widely supported.

Overcoming Listening Barriers

- **Internal Distractions:** Sometimes your mind wanders, thinking about your to-do list or how to respond next. Recognize this habit and gently pull your attention back to the speaker.
- **Emotional Reactions:** If you strongly disagree, you might mentally prepare a counter-argument instead of listening. Try to stay open until the speaker finishes, then respond.
- **Assumptions and Biases:** You might dismiss someone's point because of preconceived notions. Active listening means temporarily setting aside these biases to hear them out fully.

Practice Techniques

1. **Mirror Back Key Points:** If a friend says, "I'm worried about passing my exam," you might respond, "So you're anxious because you feel unprepared for the exam?" This invites them to clarify or confirm.
2. **Validation:** Even if you disagree, you can validate emotions: "I see that you're upset," or "It sounds like this situation is really frustrating for you."
3. **Silence is Okay:** Short pauses can encourage the speaker to continue or gather their thoughts. Resist the urge to fill every second with your own words.

Active listening strengthens your communication by making it a two-way street, not just an exchange of monologues. When you genuinely listen, you show empathy and understanding. Over time, this builds mutual respect and paves the way for deeper, more meaningful conversations.

Section 4: Giving and Receiving Feedback

Feedback is a critical part of growth, both for individuals and teams. Whether you're giving feedback—like telling a friend what you think of their presentation—or receiving feedback—like hearing from a teacher about your essay—how you handle this exchange matters a lot.

How to Give Constructive Feedback

1. **Be Specific and Objective:** Instead of saying "Your artwork is weird," you might say, "I notice the colors are very dark, which makes the mood intense. Is that the effect you wanted?" Focus on observable details rather than vague judgments.
2. **Use a Positive-First Approach:** Start by mentioning something you appreciate or find well-done. Then address areas that could be improved. This approach keeps the other person open rather than defensive.
3. **Offer Suggestions, Not Commands:** If you see a way to improve, phrase it as a suggestion: "Maybe you could try a lighter color palette?" instead of "You should never use dark colors like that."
4. **Mind Your Tone:** The same words can feel harsh or kind depending on how you say them. A calm, supportive tone conveys that you want to help, not attack.

How to Receive Feedback Gracefully

1. **Stay Open-Minded:** Even if the feedback is hard to hear, there might be truth in it. Don't let pride or fear stop you from learning.
2. **Listen Actively:** Instead of formulating defensive arguments in your mind, focus on understanding the feedback fully. Ask clarifying questions if needed.

3. **Separate Yourself from the Critique:** Realize that criticism of your work or performance is not a personal attack on your worth as a human being.
4. **Assess Before You Accept or Reject:** Not all feedback will be equally valid or useful. After hearing it, take time to evaluate if it fits your situation. You might adopt some parts and discard others.
5. **Thank the Person:** Even if you don't agree fully, thank them for taking the time to give you their perspective. This keeps the relationship respectful and open for future dialogue.

Challenges of Feedback

- **Emotional Reactions:** You might feel upset, embarrassed, or defensive when criticized. Recognize these feelings and manage them calmly. Breathe deeply, and remind yourself that feedback is often meant to help.
- **Poorly Delivered Feedback:** Sometimes, people give feedback in an unhelpful way—maybe they're too harsh or don't offer specifics. You can still glean some benefit by focusing on what's useful and ignoring the rude delivery.
- **Cultural Differences:** In some cultures, feedback is given very directly; in others, it's softened with polite language. Being aware of these differences can help you interpret and give feedback more effectively.

Long-Term Impact

When feedback is handled well, it creates an environment of continuous improvement and trust. People feel safe to take creative risks because they know mistakes can be discussed and fixed without humiliation. Regular, constructive feedback cycles can accelerate growth in personal projects, schoolwork, sports, or workplace tasks. Ultimately, it's about helping each other become better, one conversation at a time.

Section 5: Resolving Conflict Without Aggression

No matter how clear or respectful your communication, conflicts will sometimes arise. Two people may have different wants, needs, or views that clash. The key is learning to address these conflicts in a way that doesn't harm relationships or escalate into hostility.

Common Causes of Conflict

1. **Miscommunication:** One person says something ambiguous or forgets to convey vital information. Another misreads or mishears it. Small misunderstandings can grow if not addressed quickly.
2. **Different Interests or Goals:** Perhaps two siblings want to use the TV at the same time for different purposes. Or, in a work environment, team members might compete for limited resources.
3. **Emotional Buildup:** If someone feels hurt or unacknowledged for a long time, resentment builds. A minor incident can trigger a large outburst due to accumulated negative feelings.

Steps to Handle Conflict Peacefully

1. **Stay Calm:** Take a deep breath or even step away for a moment if you feel anger rising. High emotions often lead to words you might regret later.
2. **Listen to Understand:** Let the other person explain their viewpoint. Show empathy by acknowledging their feelings. This alone can defuse tension because they see you genuinely care.
3. **Share Your Perspective Factually:** Use "I" statements to describe how you feel: "I feel upset when the chores are left undone, because it affects my schedule." This approach focuses on the behavior rather than attacking the person.
4. **Seek Common Ground:** Ask, "What do we both want out of this?" Maybe both siblings want to relax after a long day, or both coworkers want the project to succeed. Identifying mutual goals can unite you.

5. **Brainstorm Solutions:** Work together to come up with ways to satisfy both needs. For instance, siblings might agree on a schedule for TV use. Coworkers might divide tasks so each can use the resources fairly.
6. **Agree on a Plan and Follow Up:** Choose a solution and see how it works. Check back after some time to ensure both sides feel the conflict is resolved.

Avoiding Unproductive Tactics

- **Name-Calling or Insults:** These immediately destroy respect and typically cause the other person to dig in or lash back.
- **Bringing Up Old Grudges:** Focus on the current issue. Resurrecting past conflicts only clouds the situation.
- **Ultimatums:** "Do this or else" statements rarely foster true cooperation. They might produce compliance out of fear but can breed resentment.

Constructive Disagreement

It's possible to disagree with someone without damaging the relationship. Present your view, listen to theirs, and accept that sometimes you won't fully agree. As long as mutual respect remains, you can still get along or find workable compromises. This mindset allows you to see conflict as an opportunity to learn about yourself and others, growing stronger together rather than drifting apart.

Section 6: Navigating Digital Communication

In today's world, much of our interaction happens via phone calls, texts, emails, or social media. While digital platforms offer convenience and speed, they also introduce unique challenges. Words on a screen lack tone of voice, facial expressions, and body language, which can lead to misunderstandings or even online hostility.

Best Practices for Texting and Messaging

1. **Be Clear and Concise:** Since typed conversations lack vocal cues, clarity is crucial. Short, incomplete phrases might be misread.
2. **Use Appropriate Emojis or Tone Indicators:** Emojis can help convey emotion (e.g., a friendly smiley face). But don't rely on them to replace actual words if the message is important.
3. **Re-Read Before Sending:** Once you hit "send," your words are out there. Skim your message for any unintentional harshness or confusing phrasing.
4. **Don't Expect Instant Replies:** Remember that people have their own schedules. If they don't respond immediately, it doesn't mean they're ignoring you.

Email Etiquette

1. **Use a Clear Subject Line:** Summarize the main point of your email so the recipient knows what to expect.
2. **Professional Tone for Formal Situations:** If you're emailing a teacher, potential employer, or someone you don't know well, use polite greetings ("Dear Mr. Smith") and a sign-off ("Sincerely" or "Best regards").
3. **Keep It Organized:** Use paragraphs for different points. A wall of text is harder to read and might cause the recipient to miss crucial details.
4. **Promptness and Politeness:** Respond in a timely manner if possible, and always maintain respect, even if you're addressing a disagreement.

Social Media Courtesy

1. **Think Before You Post:** Once something is online, it can spread quickly. Avoid sharing content that might be offensive, misleading, or too personal.
2. **Engage Positively:** If you disagree with a post, try to respond calmly. Avoid aggressive language or personal attacks. You can also consider taking the conversation to a private channel if it's complex.

3. **Respect Privacy:** Some people prefer not to be tagged in pictures or personal stories without their permission. Check first, especially if it's a sensitive topic.

Handling Online Conflicts

- **Stay Calm:** Just like in-person arguments, letting emotions take over can escalate things. Breathe, think, and respond carefully.
- **Consider Logging Off:** If a conversation becomes too heated, you can step away for a bit to gather your thoughts. Constant back-and-forth in anger usually solves nothing.
- **When to Block or Report:** If someone is harassing or threatening you, or posting extremely inappropriate content, consider blocking them or reporting the behavior to the platform.

Balancing Online and Offline

While digital communication is useful, it doesn't replace face-to-face interactions. Tone, warmth, and empathy are often easier to convey in person or over a video call. Strive for a healthy mix of online and offline conversations. This balance ensures you develop strong interpersonal skills and avoid the pitfalls of purely digital communication.

Section 7: Continuous Growth in Communication Skills

Becoming a better communicator is an ongoing process. Even expert speakers and top negotiators continue to refine their approaches. Embracing a mindset of continuous learning ensures that you keep improving your ability to connect with others.

Self-Evaluation

1. **Reflect After Key Interactions:** Did you handle a family disagreement calmly? Could you have explained your viewpoint

better in a class presentation? Think about how it went and what you can improve.
2. **Keep a Communication Journal:** Once in a while, jot down notes on challenging conversations—who was involved, what the issue was, how you responded, and what the outcome was. Over time, you'll spot patterns and areas needing attention.

Seeking Feedback

1. **Ask for Input:** Don't be afraid to ask friends, family, or mentors, "Was I clear in that discussion?" or "Do you feel I listened to you well?" Their insights can highlight blind spots.
2. **Watch Others' Reactions:** If someone seems confused or upset, it might be a sign that your message wasn't delivered as you intended. Be observant and adjust your approach.

Learning from Role Models

1. **Observe Good Communicators:** Pay attention to teachers, public speakers, or even characters on TV who communicate effectively. Notice how they phrase things, how they use pauses, or how they handle disagreements.
2. **Emulate, Then Adapt:** You can try out techniques you admire, but be sure to adapt them to your personality. Authenticity is crucial; copying someone else's style exactly might come off as forced.

Training and Practice

1. **Join Clubs or Workshops:** Activities like debate club, drama group, or public speaking courses can build confidence and hone your speaking and listening skills.
2. **Use Tech Tools:** Practice recording yourself reading a script or giving a short speech. Listening to the playback can reveal issues with pacing, clarity, or tone that you didn't notice in the moment.

Patience with Yourself

As you experiment with different strategies, you'll have successes and failures. You might slip back into old habits under stress or become flustered in challenging conversations. That's normal. Each setback is another chance to refine your skills. Communicating clearly and respectfully is a lifelong journey, one that evolves with each new experience and context.

The Bigger Picture

When you invest in improving your communication skills, you enhance not just your own life but also the lives of those around you. Clear, respectful exchanges can reduce conflicts, build deeper connections, and create collaborative environments in school, work, and personal relationships. Over time, these positive interactions can ripple out into broader society, helping to foster more understanding and empathy among individuals, groups, and communities alike.

Chapter 16: Facing Stress and Anxiety

Introduction

Everyone experiences stress and anxiety at times. A big exam, a job interview, conflicts with friends, or sudden changes in life circumstances can all trigger these feelings. While occasional stress and mild anxiety can push us to perform better or solve problems, chronic or overwhelming levels can harm our physical health, mental well-being, and relationships.

In this chapter, we will explore practical strategies for **facing stress and anxiety**. We'll talk about understanding what triggers these emotions, how to spot the warning signs in your mind and body, and how to cope in healthy ways. You'll learn about daily habits that build resilience—like exercise, relaxation techniques, and time management. We'll also look at ways to calm yourself during moments of intense stress or panic, whether through mindfulness, deep breathing, or positive self-talk.

Furthermore, we'll discuss the difference between normal anxiety—such as feeling nervous before a performance—and more severe anxiety conditions that might need professional help. Recognizing when you or someone else needs extra support is part of taking responsibility for your mental health.

By the end of this chapter, you'll have a toolkit of methods to handle stressors and anxieties that come your way. Whether you're a student, a working adult, or simply someone who wants to live with less tension, these tools can help you navigate life more smoothly and confidently. Let's begin by understanding the nature of stress and anxiety and how they affect our minds and bodies.

Section 1: Understanding Stress and Anxiety

Stress and anxiety often get mentioned together, but they're slightly different. **Stress** is generally a response to an external demand or challenge—like a tight deadline or a family argument. **Anxiety**, on the other hand, can persist even when there's no clear external trigger. It involves worry about potential future threats or unknown outcomes.

How They Affect Your Body and Mind

1. **Physical Responses:** You might notice muscle tension, headaches, a racing heart, or an upset stomach. Chronic stress or high anxiety can weaken your immune system, making you more prone to illnesses.
2. **Emotional and Mental Effects:** Stress can lead to frustration or irritability, while anxiety often results in persistent worry or fear. Both can cause trouble sleeping, concentration issues, or forgetfulness.
3. **Behavioral Changes:** Overwhelming stress or anxiety might prompt unhealthy coping, like overeating, smoking, or withdrawing from social activities. It can also trigger mood swings or a short temper, impacting relationships.

Positive vs. Negative Stress

Sometimes, a bit of stress—often called "eustress"—can motivate you to prepare for a test or meet a deadline. It can feel exciting, like before a big game or performance. However, "distress" refers to overwhelming, harmful stress. Recognizing which type you're experiencing helps you respond appropriately.

Common Triggers

- **Major Life Changes:** Moving to a new city, starting a new job, or going through a breakup.

- **Academic or Work Pressures:** Exams, projects, deadlines, or performance evaluations.
- **Relationship Conflicts:** Fights with friends, family tensions, or romantic issues.
- **Financial Strain:** Worrying about bills, debts, or job security.
- **Health Concerns:** Illnesses or worrying about potential medical problems.

Why Some People Are More Prone

Everyone's tolerance for stress varies based on genetics, upbringing, and life experience. Some individuals naturally stay calmer under pressure, while others become anxious more quickly. Past traumas or high-stress childhood environments can also make the mind and body more sensitive to threats or uncertainties.

When Anxiety Becomes a Disorder

Feeling nervous before a big event is normal. However, if anxiety is persistent, intense, and interferes with daily life—like stopping you from going outside or making you unable to focus at school or work—you might have an anxiety disorder. Conditions such as generalized anxiety disorder, panic disorder, or social anxiety disorder often require professional guidance. It's important to note that seeking help is not a sign of weakness; it's a responsible step toward better health.

The Importance of Awareness

The first step in managing stress and anxiety is understanding how they manifest in your life. By noticing your physical symptoms, emotional cues, and triggers, you become more empowered to take proactive measures. The goal is not to eliminate stress or anxiety completely—some level of stress is inevitable—but to keep them at manageable levels so you can function and thrive.

Section 2: Identifying Your Personal Warning Signs

Not everyone experiences stress and anxiety in the same way. One person might get headaches, another might have trouble sleeping, and someone else might become withdrawn or irritable. Recognizing your own warning signs is key to catching stress or anxiety before it escalates.

Physical Indicators

1. **Tense Muscles or Clenched Jaw:** You might unconsciously grip your jaw or tense your shoulders when anxious. Over time, this can lead to chronic pain.
2. **Changes in Appetite:** Some people overeat when stressed, seeking comfort in food, while others lose their appetite.
3. **Rapid Heartbeat or Sweating:** A sudden increase in heart rate, sweaty palms, or feeling flushed can be stress signals.
4. **Frequent Illnesses:** Chronic stress can deplete your immune system. If you're catching colds repeatedly, stress might be contributing.

Emotional and Mental Signs

1. **Irritability or Mood Swings:** You may snap at people more easily or feel unexplainably grumpy.
2. **Difficulty Concentrating:** Stress often jumbles your thoughts, making it hard to stay on task.
3. **Restlessness and Racing Thoughts:** Anxiety might cause your mind to jump from one worry to another, leaving you unable to focus on daily activities.
4. **Feeling Overwhelmed or Hopeless:** You might sense that no matter what you do, you can't keep up with life's demands. This can feed into a cycle of negative thinking.

Behavioral Clues

1. **Procrastination or Avoidance:** Putting off tasks because they feel too stressful. This often worsens the cycle, as things pile up.
2. **Social Withdrawal:** You may skip gatherings or ignore phone calls because you feel too anxious to face people.
3. **Overcommitting:** Interestingly, some people do the opposite—taking on too many tasks to distract themselves from worries, which eventually leads to more stress.
4. **Reliance on Substances:** Reaching for cigarettes, alcohol, or other substances as a coping mechanism is a major sign that stress or anxiety is going unchecked.

Keeping a Stress/Anxiety Journal

A helpful technique is to maintain a small notebook or use an app to log when you feel stressed or anxious. Write down:

- The date and time.
- The situation you were in.
- Physical symptoms (e.g., headache, sweaty palms).
- Emotional state (e.g., nervous, upset, angry).
- How you responded or coped.

Over time, patterns will emerge—like certain days, situations, or triggers. Recognizing these is the first step to effective management. For instance, you might realize you get anxious every Monday morning or before specific meetings.

Importance of Early Detection

If you identify warning signs early—like noticing you're tense or snapping at people—you can apply stress-management techniques (such as deep breathing or taking a quick walk) to prevent escalation. Early intervention often means simpler solutions. If you wait until stress or anxiety is overwhelming, you might need more extensive help, and the impact on your health or relationships could be greater.

By honing your awareness of physical, emotional, and behavioral cues, you regain some control over stress and anxiety. It's like noticing the storm clouds before the rain pours, giving you time to grab an umbrella. That "umbrella" can be any number of coping strategies, which we'll explore in the next sections.

Section 3: Daily Habits to Build Resilience

Building resilience means developing the ability to bounce back from challenges and stressors. This doesn't happen overnight; it's cultivated through consistent, healthy habits that strengthen your mind and body over time. Think of it like training for a marathon—you need to prepare well before the race day stress hits.

1. Regular Exercise

1. **Physical Benefits:** Activities like walking, jogging, swimming, or dancing lower stress hormones and release endorphins (the "feel-good" chemicals).
2. **Mental Boost:** Exercise can clear your head, improve mood, and increase confidence in your capabilities.
3. **Routine Matters:** Aim for at least 20–30 minutes of moderate exercise most days of the week. Even short 10-minute sessions can help if you're busy.

2. Balanced Diet

1. **Fueling Your Brain:** Nutritious foods high in vitamins, minerals, and healthy fats support brain function. Junk food might give short-term comfort but doesn't help your body cope long-term.
2. **Stable Energy:** Sugary snacks can lead to energy spikes and crashes, intensifying anxiety. Whole grains, lean proteins, fruits, and vegetables provide steady energy.

3. Adequate Sleep

1. **Rest for Repair:** During deep sleep, your body and mind recover from daily wear and tear. Lack of sleep increases irritability and reduces your ability to handle stress.
2. **Bedtime Routine:** Set a regular schedule, avoid caffeine late in the day, and limit screen time before bed. This improves the quality of your rest.

4. Mindful Breathing and Relaxation

1. **Breathing Techniques:** Inhale slowly through your nose for a count of four, hold for four, then exhale through your mouth for four. Repeat several times. This slows your heart rate and calms your nerves.
2. **Progressive Muscle Relaxation:** Tense and relax different muscle groups in your body, moving from your toes up to your head. Notice the contrast between tension and relaxation.

5. Time Management

1. **Plan Your Day:** Having a clear schedule can reduce last-minute stress.
2. **Set Priorities:** Identify what tasks are urgent and which can wait. Trying to do everything at once creates unnecessary pressure.
3. **Break Tasks Down:** If an assignment feels overwhelming, divide it into smaller steps. This makes your goal more approachable.

6. Social Support

1. **Stay Connected:** Good relationships can buffer against stress. Sharing worries or seeking advice from friends or family can lighten your emotional load.
2. **Team Up for Activities:** Exercising, cooking, or studying with someone can make tasks more fun and less daunting.

7. Positive Outlook

1. **Gratitude Practice:** Recall or write down a few things you're thankful for each day. This keeps you from focusing only on problems.
2. **Self-Encouragement:** Notice your successes, even the small ones. Acknowledge the effort you're putting in.

When you weave these habits into your daily life, you build a strong foundation. Resilience doesn't mean you'll never feel stress or anxiety again, but it does mean you'll recover faster and handle challenges with greater poise. Over weeks and months of consistent practice, you'll likely see changes in your mood, energy levels, and overall sense of well-being.

Section 4: Calming Techniques for Immediate Stress Relief

Sometimes stress or anxiety hits suddenly—a panic before a speech, a wave of worry late at night, or a surge of tension after an argument. In these moments, you need quick coping strategies to help you calm down and think clearly.

1. Deep Breathing Exercises

1. **4-7-8 Method:** Breathe in for four seconds, hold your breath for seven seconds, then exhale slowly for eight seconds. Repeat several times. This technique slows your heart rate and promotes relaxation.
2. **Box Breathing:** Inhale for a count of four, hold for four, exhale for four, and hold again for four before the next inhale. Visualize a box with each side representing one part of the breath cycle.

2. Grounding Yourself

1. **5-4-3-2-1 Technique:** Identify five things you can see, four you can touch, three you can hear, two you can smell, and one you can taste (or recall a taste). This anchors you in the present moment, shifting focus from anxious thoughts to immediate sensory details.
2. **Name the Emotion:** Quietly say to yourself, "I'm feeling anxious" or "I'm feeling angry." Recognizing the emotion can lessen its intensity and give you a sense of control.

3. Quick Distractions

1. **Movement:** Get up and stretch, walk around the block, or do a quick set of jumping jacks. Physical activity redirects nervous energy.
2. **Engage a Sense:** Sipping cold water, smelling a soothing essential oil, or chewing mint gum can disrupt spiraling anxious thoughts.

4. Self-Talk

1. **Positive Affirmations:** Remind yourself, "I've overcome challenges before. I can do it again," or "This feeling is temporary. I will get through it."
2. **Reassure Yourself:** If you're panicking about an upcoming event, remind yourself you've prepared. Say, "I studied well for this test. I'm ready to try my best."

5. Mini-Meditation

1. **One-Minute Focus:** Close your eyes, take slow breaths, and observe your inhalations and exhalations. If thoughts drift, gently bring them back to your breathing. Even a short session can calm racing thoughts.
2. **Mantra Repetition:** Repeat a calming phrase like "I am safe, I am calm" in your mind. This blocks out anxious chatter.

6. Progressive Relaxation (Quick Version)

If you don't have time for a full muscle relaxation routine, quickly tense and release major muscle groups: fists, shoulders, and face. Notice the release of tension, which can ease overall stress.

The Key: Practice Regularly

These techniques might feel awkward at first, especially when you're under pressure. Practicing them during calm moments can make them more effective in stressful situations. Over time, your body learns to recognize these methods as signals to relax. You might not eliminate your stress entirely, but you'll reduce it enough to think more rationally, make better decisions, or simply ride out the wave of anxiety until it passes.

Section 5: Long-Term Strategies for Managing Anxiety

While immediate calming techniques are vital, long-term anxiety management often requires deeper changes in lifestyle, mindset, and self-awareness. If you find yourself struggling with chronic worry or fear, consider incorporating these strategies into your routine.

1. Cognitive Behavioral Techniques

1. **Identify Negative Thought Patterns:** Anxiety often comes from thinking "worst-case scenario" or exaggerating threats. Write down anxious thoughts and challenge their reality.
2. **Replace with Balanced Thoughts:** If your mind says, "I'll fail this exam," counter with, "I've studied, and I'm prepared to do my best. Even if I don't get an A, I can learn from my mistakes."
3. **Work with a Therapist:** A mental health professional trained in Cognitive Behavioral Therapy (CBT) can guide you through exercises tailored to your specific anxiety triggers.

2. Gradual Exposure

1. **Facing Fears in Small Steps:** If you fear public speaking, start by talking in front of a mirror, then try speaking to one friend, then a small group, and finally a larger audience.
2. **Praise Progress:** Each step you take to confront your anxiety—no matter how minor—is progress worth celebrating.

3. Mindfulness and Meditation

1. **Daily Practice:** Spending 5–10 minutes each day focusing on your breath or a mantra can help you develop a calmer baseline.
2. **Observing Thoughts:** Instead of getting tangled in anxious thoughts, observe them like clouds passing in the sky. Recognize they're thoughts, not absolute truths.

4. Time-Management Skills

1. **Set Realistic Goals:** Overloaded schedules can exacerbate anxiety. Aim for a balanced approach to work, study, and leisure.
2. **Learn to Say "No":** If you're prone to worry, taking on too many responsibilities can elevate stress. Politely declining extra tasks helps protect your mental health.

5. Social Support Networks

1. **Trusted Friends or Family:** Talking about worries reduces their power. Sharing what's on your mind can provide relief and sometimes helpful perspectives.
2. **Support Groups or Forums:** Meeting people with similar experiences can be comforting. You realize you're not alone, and you can learn coping methods from others.

6. Professional Help

1. **Therapists and Counselors:** They can teach coping strategies, help you understand anxiety triggers, and guide you through tough life transitions.

2. **Medication:** In some cases, doctors may recommend anxiety medication. Always consult a health professional before taking any prescription to discuss benefits and risks.

7. Continuous Self-Monitoring

- **Regular Check-Ins:** Note how you feel each day or week. Are you less anxious after adopting these habits? If not, consider adjusting your approach or seeking additional help.
- **Celebrate Milestones:** Recognizing your progress—like going a week without a panic attack—reinforces positive behavior. Keep track of these victories to motivate yourself.

Long-term anxiety management isn't about removing all fear from your life. Instead, it's about living fully despite worries, staying grounded in reality, and taking proactive steps whenever anxiety starts to interfere. With consistent effort, you'll discover that many anxious feelings lose their intensity, allowing you to pursue goals and enjoy relationships with greater calm and confidence.

Section 6: Knowing When to Seek Professional Help

While self-help strategies are valuable, sometimes anxiety or stress levels go beyond what you can handle alone. Recognizing the signs that professional intervention is needed can save you from prolonged suffering and complications down the road.

Signs You Might Need Extra Support

1. **Persistent Symptoms:** If you've tried multiple coping strategies for weeks or months but still struggle daily with intense anxiety or stress, consider seeking help.

2. **Interference with Daily Life:** You might find it hard to concentrate in class, complete work tasks, or maintain relationships because of your worry or stress.
3. **Physical Symptoms:** Severe stress can lead to frequent headaches, stomach issues, or sleepless nights that don't improve with lifestyle changes.
4. **Isolation or Despair:** If you're withdrawing from friends, family, or activities you used to enjoy, or if you experience persistent hopelessness, it's time to consult a professional.
5. **Excessive Fear or Panic Attacks:** Recurrent panic attacks or fears (like fear of crowds, social gatherings, or specific objects) may indicate an anxiety disorder.

Types of Professionals Who Can Help

1. **Therapists or Counselors (Licensed Professional Counselor, Clinical Psychologist):** They provide talk therapy methods such as CBT, which can help reframe negative thoughts and teach coping skills.
2. **Psychiatrists (Medical Doctors):** They can diagnose mental health conditions and prescribe medication if necessary.
3. **Primary Care Doctors:** Sometimes, physical conditions like thyroid problems can mimic anxiety. A general check-up can rule out underlying medical causes.
4. **School Counselors or College Mental Health Services:** If you're a student, these resources are often available at no or low cost.

Overcoming Stigma or Fear

1. **Mental Health is Health:** Seeking help for emotional distress is no different from seeing a doctor for a broken bone. It's a responsible step toward healing.
2. **Confidentiality:** Therapists and mental health professionals are bound by privacy rules. They won't share your details unless there's a concern about your immediate safety or someone else's.
3. **You're Not Weak:** Accepting that you need support shows courage and self-awareness. It's a sign you respect yourself enough to seek care.

What to Expect in Therapy

1. **Initial Assessment:** The therapist asks about your symptoms, history, and concerns.
2. **Goal Setting:** Together, you identify what you hope to achieve—like reducing panic attacks, improving your ability to socialize, or handling stress better.
3. **Regular Sessions:** You might meet weekly or biweekly to discuss progress, learn new techniques, and refine existing coping strategies.
4. **Homework or Exercises:** Therapists often give tasks between sessions, like journaling or practicing relaxation methods.

The Results

Many people find that professional help, combined with self-care, improves their outlook significantly. They learn to manage stress and anxiety, maintain healthier relationships, and restore confidence in their own abilities to navigate life's ups and downs. If you feel you've tried a variety of self-help methods without improvement, remember that reaching out for professional support is a valid and often life-changing choice.

Chapter 17: Balancing Work and Personal Life

Introduction

In a busy world full of responsibilities—from school or work tasks to family care and personal hobbies—it's easy to feel like there just aren't enough hours in the day. Many people struggle to balance the demands of their job (or studies) with their personal lives. They might spend long hours at the office and come home too tired to enjoy time with family or relax. Or they could be a student juggling school assignments, part-time work, and social activities, all while feeling overwhelmed.

This chapter is about **balancing work and personal life**, whether "work" means an actual job, academic responsibilities, or a major personal project that requires your time. We'll explore why balance matters to your well-being and happiness, and we'll look at practical strategies to help you set boundaries, manage your time better, and keep your stress levels under control. We'll also consider how to communicate needs and limits to employers, teachers, or loved ones so that everyone understands and respects your priorities.

By the end of this chapter, you'll see that work-life balance is not about eliminating hard work from your life. Instead, it's about creating a healthier rhythm. You'll gain ideas on how to plan your schedule, protect your personal time, make the most of breaks, and keep your relationships strong. You'll also learn how to deal with common issues like burnout, guilt over not working enough, or pressure from bosses and peers. Let's discover together how a balanced approach to daily life can lead to better productivity, stronger connections with loved ones, and greater satisfaction overall.

Section 1: Why Work-Life Balance Matters

Health and Happiness

One of the biggest reasons to aim for work-life balance is health. Spending all your time on work or studies without personal breaks can lead to high stress, fatigue, and even mental health issues like anxiety or depression. On the flip side, if you neglect work or important responsibilities entirely, you might struggle with financial problems, worry about your future, or feel unfulfilled because you're not growing in your career or academic path.

A balanced approach recognizes that **both** work and personal life contribute to your overall well-being. Work can give you purpose, income, and a sense of achievement, while personal life gives you rest, fun, emotional support, and time to pursue passions or connect with loved ones. When these two parts of life are in harmony, you're more likely to feel satisfied and stable.

Productivity and Focus

Ironically, people who never take breaks or personal time can become less productive over the long run. Their mental energy gets drained, creativity declines, and mistakes occur more often. Meanwhile, those who allow themselves time to rest, socialize, or engage in hobbies often return to work with renewed energy and sharper focus. They can accomplish tasks in less time because they aren't constantly battling exhaustion or burnout.

Relationships and Support

Work-life balance also matters for relationships. If you're always working late, you might miss family dinners or lose touch with friends. Over time, that can weaken important bonds. Having personal time ensures you nurture these connections—eating together, chatting about each other's day, celebrating milestones, or offering emotional support. In turn, strong relationships serve as a safety net when work gets tough. Loved ones can provide encouragement, ideas, or even practical help, making it easier to handle challenges.

Long-Term Stability

People who consistently ignore personal life for the sake of work might experience short-term career gains, such as a promotion or extra earnings. But if they burn out or damage their health and relationships, they can face serious issues later—like having to take extended sick leave, dealing with family conflicts, or even quitting a job due to overwhelming stress. A balanced strategy aims to maintain steady progress over many years, rather than short bursts of unsustainable effort.

Emotional Well-Being

Lastly, a balanced life helps you maintain a positive emotional state. Working all day, every day, can cause you to miss out on small joys—whether it's watching a favorite show, going for a walk, practicing a hobby, or visiting relatives. These "small joys" are often crucial for mental health. They act as mini rewards that keep you going when deadlines loom or when tasks feel tedious.

When you see that balance is not just a luxury but a necessity for health, happiness, productivity, relationships, long-term stability, and emotional well-being, it becomes clear why this topic is so important. In in the next sections, we'll explore how to set boundaries, manage time, and handle the daily juggling act without feeling overwhelmed.

Section 2: Setting Boundaries Between Work and Personal Life

One of the main challenges to achieving work-life balance is **boundaries**—the line that separates professional tasks from personal space. Without clear boundaries, you might find yourself checking work emails during family gatherings or thinking about unfinished homework while out with friends. Over time, this mix-up can cause stress, reduce the quality of personal time, and lead to burnout.

and "could do" (nice-to-have or optional). This helps you see what truly requires your immediate attention.
- **Evaluate Deadlines:** Some tasks might feel urgent but aren't actually due right away. If you have multiple projects, you can tackle them in an order that makes sense, giving yourself buffer time for each.

Scheduling Techniques

- **Time Blocking:** Allocate specific blocks of time for different activities—work tasks, personal errands, exercise, or family time. When the block ends, move on to the next, even if you haven't fully finished. This trains you to work more efficiently.
- **Pomodoro Technique:** Work (or study) in 25-minute intervals, followed by a 5-minute break. After four cycles, take a longer break (15–20 minutes). This approach keeps your mind fresh.
- **Batching Similar Tasks:** Group tasks that require a similar mindset—like responding to emails, making phone calls, or doing chores—so you reduce "task-switching" time.

Managing Distractions

- **Phone Settings:** Turn off unnecessary notifications or use "Do Not Disturb" during focused work sessions. Notifications can disrupt your flow.
- **Create a Distraction-Free Environment:** This might mean working in a library, using noise-canceling headphones, or closing your office door if you have one. Let others know you're in a quiet period.
- **Limit Social Media:** Scrolling through social media can eat up hours. Set a timer or use an app that limits how much time you can spend on those platforms.

Avoiding Overcommitment

- **Learn to Say "No":** If you already have a packed schedule, don't automatically agree to another project or social event. Check your priorities and mental space first.

- **Delegate or Ask for Help**: If certain tasks can be handled by coworkers, family members, or professional services, consider delegating. Doing everything alone is not always practical.

Reflecting on Your Time

- **Weekly Review**: Each week, take a few minutes to see where your time went. Were you too busy with minor tasks and neglected important ones? Did you schedule enough breaks? An honest review helps you adjust.
- **Celebrate Small Wins**: If you managed to complete your work on time and still relax over the weekend, recognize that success. Positive reinforcement encourages you to stick with good habits.

With effective time management, you're not just working more quickly—you're working more wisely. By prioritizing important tasks, minimizing distractions, and keeping track of your time, you make room in your schedule for family, friends, hobbies, and self-care. Over time, this consistent discipline in handling tasks allows you to achieve your goals at work or school while preserving the rest and pleasure you need to stay motivated and happy.

Section 4: Dealing with Burnout and Overwork

Despite your best efforts to balance work and personal life, there may be seasons when deadlines pile up or unexpected crises occur, leading to burnout. **Burnout** is a state of physical, emotional, and mental exhaustion caused by excessive and prolonged stress. It often happens when you feel overwhelmed, emotionally drained, and unable to meet constant demands. Recognizing the signs early and taking corrective steps can prevent severe problems later.

Signs of Burnout

1. **Extreme Fatigue:** Even after sleeping, you still feel tired. This might be physical weakness or a constant mental heaviness.
2. **Cynicism or Detachment:** You might lose enthusiasm for tasks you once enjoyed, feeling distant or numb.
3. **Frequent Mistakes:** Tiredness can harm your focus. You might forget important steps or details, causing errors.
4. **Irritability:** Small inconveniences trigger big emotional reactions. You might snap at coworkers, friends, or family.
5. **Loss of Accomplishment:** You could feel like no matter what you do, it's not enough or doesn't matter. This sense of hopelessness can feed the cycle of burnout.

Common Causes

- **Excessive Work Hours:** Putting in too many hours without adequate breaks.
- **Lack of Control:** Feeling you have no say in your workload or schedule.
- **Poor Work Environment:** Unsafe or toxic atmospheres—like constant conflict, bullying, or unclear expectations.
- **High Perfectionism:** Setting unrealistic personal standards can lead to perpetual stress.
- **Emotional Demands:** Jobs or roles that require constant empathy (like caregiving) can exhaust emotional reserves if you don't replenish them.

Strategies to Recover

1. **Take a True Break:** If possible, schedule time off—vacation days, a weekend getaway, or even just a "staycation" at home with zero work tasks. Let your mind and body rest.
2. **Simplify Your Tasks:** During burnout recovery, focus on essential responsibilities only. See if you can postpone or delegate less important items.

3. **Seek Support:** Talk to a supervisor, teacher, or mentor about your situation. Sometimes, adjusting workloads or expectations can help. Share your feelings with a trusted friend or family member for emotional comfort.
4. **Practice Self-Care:** Return to basics: quality sleep, healthy meals, regular exercise, and gentle mindfulness routines. These habits help your system recover from chronic stress.
5. **Professional Help:** If burnout is severe, consult a mental health professional. A counselor can guide you to set boundaries or develop coping strategies.

Preventing Future Burnout

- **Regular Check-Ins:** Reflect weekly on your stress levels and whether you're pushing too hard.
- **Micro-Breaks:** Even a 10-minute walk or a few moments to stretch can break the cycle of nonstop work.
- **Variety in Work:** If you can, rotate tasks or change your routine to avoid monotony. Learning new skills can re-energize you.
- **Open Communication:** Keep channels open with your boss or team. If you feel workload pressures rising, mention it early before it becomes unmanageable.

Burnout doesn't just harm productivity—it can damage relationships, mental health, and overall quality of life. Recognizing its signs and taking proactive steps is vital. By making small but consistent adjustments to your workload and self-care, you can come back from burnout with a fresh perspective, renewed energy, and a healthier relationship with work.

Section 5: Nurturing Personal Life and Relationships

Balancing work and personal life isn't just about reducing stress. It's also about **positively investing in the personal side**—your hobbies, friendships, family, and mental rest. If you only reduce work hours but don't fill that time with meaningful or restful activities, you might not experience the full benefits of balance. In this section, we'll look at ways to nurture relationships and personal interests so your free time truly revitalizes you.

Quality Over Quantity

- **Intentional Time with Loved Ones:** Spending three fully engaged hours with family (where you put your phone aside, have real conversations, and share experiences) can be more rewarding than eight hours of being physically present but mentally elsewhere.
- **Focused Communication:** Ask open-ended questions like "How was your day?" or "What did you learn at school/work?" Listen actively, show empathy, and let them feel heard.

Shared Activities

- **Cooking Together:** Making a meal with family or friends can be fun, and you also get to eat the results.
- **Game Nights or Movie Nights:** Simple but effective ways to bond. Rotate who picks the game or film to keep everyone involved.
- **Outdoor Adventures:** Picnics, hikes, or casual sports sessions help you get fresh air and exercise while connecting with others.

Personal Hobbies and Passions

- **Creative Outlets:** Drawing, painting, crafting, writing, or playing an instrument can reduce stress and spark joy. Even 15 minutes a day can rekindle creativity.
- **Physical Recreation:** Dancing, yoga, or any form of movement can lift your mood. It doesn't have to be intense—just something you find fun.
- **Learning New Skills:** Trying a new language, taking an online course, or exploring a tech hobby can expand your horizons and keep your mind active.

Alone Time and Self-Care

- **Recharge Solo:** Some people need quiet, alone moments to recharge. Reading a book, listening to music, or doing a puzzle can help you unwind without any social demands.
- **Mindfulness or Meditation:** Spending a few minutes focusing on your breathing or silently observing your thoughts can reduce mental clutter.
- **Journaling:** Writing down feelings, experiences, or small daily successes can offer mental clarity and emotional release.

Saying "Yes" to Fun

- **Embrace Spontaneity:** While planning helps, sometimes you need to seize unexpected moments—like spontaneously going for ice cream or meeting a friend for a quick chat. These small, joyful decisions can lighten your mood.
- **Avoid Guilt:** If you've scheduled personal time, enjoy it without feeling bad about not working. Guilt undermines the relaxation you're trying to achieve.
- **Celebrate Achievements:** Whether it's finishing a project at work or your child scoring a goal in a soccer match, take a moment to celebrate together. Recognizing wins (big or small) adds positivity to personal life.

When you actively nurture relationships, hobbies, and rest, you restore the emotional energy you spend at work or school. This not only prevents burnout but also enhances your capacity to handle responsibilities. A fulfilling personal life becomes a buffer against stress, reminding you there's more to life than just deadlines and to-do lists. Over time, you'll find that a richer personal domain actually makes you more effective, satisfied, and resilient in your professional or academic roles.

Section 6: Communicating Needs and Setting Expectations

Balancing work and personal life is often a group effort. Coworkers, bosses, teachers, family members, or friends can either support your boundaries or unintentionally make them harder to uphold. That's why **communicating your needs and setting clear expectations** is so important.

Telling Your Employer or Teacher

- **Be Proactive:** If you have an exam date or an important family event coming, inform your boss or teacher early. This way, they can schedule tasks or deadlines accordingly, reducing last-minute surprises.
- **Suggest Solutions:** Instead of simply saying, "I need time off," propose options: "I can work an extra hour each day earlier in the week so I can leave early on Friday." Offering alternatives shows responsibility and willingness to compromise.
- **Explain Your Limits:** If you're consistently asked to work overtime, calmly express that you need to maintain personal time. You could say, "I want to give my best at work, but I also need to rest and handle family responsibilities."

Discussing Boundaries with Family and Friends

- **Clarify Your Schedule:** If you need certain hours for uninterrupted work or study, tell your family. Post a copy of your schedule or add it to a family calendar.
- **Ask for Respectful Communication:** Let friends know that last-minute gatherings might be hard to attend if you have a tight schedule. Suggest planning outings in advance.
- **Offer Explanations Without Apologies:** You don't have to be sorry for having personal or work obligations. You can say, "I'd love to join you, but this Saturday I really need to finish a project. Let's aim for next weekend!"

Handling Pushback

Sometimes, people around you may resist or not understand your boundaries. Maybe a boss expects 24/7 availability, or a friend guilt-trips you for missing a party.

- **Stay Firm but Polite:** Restate your boundaries calmly. For example, "I'm sorry, but I'm not available after 8 PM for work calls. I can address any urgent issues first thing in the morning."
- **Compromise When Possible:** If it's a one-time special event, you might adapt your boundary slightly—like answering a crucial work call in the evening. But keep these exceptions rare, so you don't set a precedent of being always on call.
- **Offer Empathy:** Sometimes, the other person is under pressure too. If a coworker demands an immediate response, they might be facing their own deadline. Show you understand, but also remind them of your limits.

Approaching Conflict Constructively

- **Use "I" Statements:** Instead of accusing the other person, focus on how you feel. "I feel stressed when I receive calls late at night," invites understanding rather than blame.
- **Listen to Their Side:** They might have reasons for their requests. Listening doesn't mean you give in, but it can lead to a more balanced solution.
- **Stay Solution-Oriented:** If your boss needs coverage, maybe you can find a rotating schedule with coworkers rather than always having you fill in.

By clearly stating your needs and being open to dialogue, you can reduce conflicts and teach others how to respect your limits. This not only preserves your personal time but also builds a culture of mutual respect and cooperation—whether in the workplace, classroom, or home environment.

Chapter 18: Adapting to Change

Introduction

Change is inevitable. Whether it's moving to a new home, switching schools, starting a new job, or facing a major shift in your personal life, change can be both exciting and frightening. Some people thrive on variety and adventure, while others prefer stability and find sudden alterations to their routine stressful. Regardless of your preference, developing skills to **adapt to change** is crucial for personal growth, emotional well-being, and long-term success in a fast-paced world.

In this chapter, we'll explore how to recognize different types of change—like planned changes (such as going to college) or unexpected ones (like losing a job or dealing with a health issue). We'll discuss ways to handle the emotional impact of change, including anxiety and fear of the unknown. You'll learn practical strategies for staying flexible, managing stress, and discovering the opportunities that change often brings. We'll also examine how to communicate with those around you during transitional times, ensuring that relationships remain supportive and understanding.

By the end of this chapter, you'll see that adaptation doesn't mean giving up your identity or values. Instead, it's about maintaining a balance between what you hold dear and what you must adjust to meet new circumstances. Through flexibility, an open mind, and strong coping mechanisms, you can transform challenging changes into possibilities for learning and improvement. Let's dive into the nature of change, why it can feel so overwhelming, and how you can remain steady (yet adaptable) when life's winds shift course.

Section 1: Understanding Why Change Feels Hard

Our Comfort Zone

Humans naturally seek comfort and predictability. We develop routines—like waking up at the same time, traveling familiar roads to work or school, and interacting with the same circle of friends. These habits give us a sense of control. When something disrupts these routines—like transferring to a new department or relocating to a different city—we may feel uneasy. This discomfort arises from stepping out of our **comfort zone**, a mental space where we feel safe because the environment is familiar.

Fear of the Unknown

Change often involves uncertainty. If you're starting a new job, you don't yet know your coworkers, the office culture, or even where to find supplies. If you're moving to a new city, you might fear being lonely or not finding your way around. **Uncertainty** triggers worry: "What if I fail?" or "What if people don't like me?" Our brains prefer situations with clear expectations, so facing something unclear can spark anxiety.

Emotional Attachments

Sometimes, resisting change comes from not wanting to lose what we currently have. If you love your old house, leaving it behind can be painful, even if the new place is bigger or in a better neighborhood. If you're close to your coworkers, switching jobs can feel like losing a group of friends. These emotional attachments make transitions difficult. While we might logically know the change is positive, our emotions mourn what we're leaving behind.

Loss of Familiar Skills or Status

When you're experienced in your role or comfortable in your academic environment, change can force you to feel like a beginner again. For instance, a promotion might offer more money and responsibility but also requires learning new skills quickly. If you're used to being the "expert," it's unsettling to return to a learning phase. Similarly, switching schools means losing seniority or friendships you've built over time.

Social Pressure

People around you might react to your changes in different ways. Some might be happy for you; others might be jealous or worried about losing your company. If you sense disapproval or skepticism from friends or relatives, it can add stress. You might feel torn between moving forward and maintaining relationships.

Past Negative Experiences

If you've gone through a tough change before—like a messy breakup or a failed job attempt—your mind might associate all changes with those bad feelings. This can lead to hesitance or fear of repeating negative experiences. Overcoming these mental blocks often requires recognizing that each situation is unique and that past outcomes don't dictate the future.

By understanding these aspects—comfort zones, fear of the unknown, emotional attachments, skill concerns, social pressure, and past experiences—you can see why change triggers complex emotions. Recognizing why you feel uneasy is the first step to managing those feelings. In the next sections, we'll explore how to handle the emotional wave that often accompanies major life shifts and ways to turn change into an opportunity rather than a threat.

Section 2: Emotional Responses to Change—and How to Cope

Recognizing Your Emotions

When change happens, you may feel a wide range of emotions—excitement, fear, sadness, anticipation, or even anger.

Identifying these feelings can help you cope. Instead of saying, "I'm just stressed," try to be specific: "I feel nervous because I don't know my new coworkers," or "I'm sad about leaving my friend group." Naming emotions gives you clarity about what's bothering you.

Managing Anxiety and Worry

1. **Deep Breathing:** When anxiety spikes, take slow, deep breaths. Focus on the rhythm of your inhales and exhales to calm your racing thoughts.
2. **Write Down Concerns:** Putting worries on paper can reduce their intensity. List possible solutions or steps to address each concern, which makes them feel more controllable.
3. **Perspective Check:** Ask yourself, "Will this change matter a year from now?" or "What's the worst that could happen, and how would I handle it?" Often, the worst-case scenario is still manageable.

Grief and Letting Go

Change sometimes involves saying goodbye—to a place, a routine, or people. It's natural to grieve what you're leaving behind. This process can include sadness, nostalgia, and even regret. Let yourself feel these emotions without shame. You can commemorate what you're losing—take photos, write down memories, or share stories with friends—so you can move forward without feeling like you've just erased your past.

Embracing Excitement and Curiosity

Not all feelings around change are negative. There might be a spark of excitement about new opportunities, fresh surroundings, or learning a skill you never had a chance to develop. Try to balance your worries with curiosity: "What new experiences might I enjoy?" or "Who might I meet in this new situation?" Letting yourself be a bit adventurous can reduce the heaviness of fear.

Seeking Emotional Support

1. **Talk to Friends or Family:** Sometimes just sharing your thoughts out loud helps you feel better and gather new ideas.
2. **Professional Help:** If you experience overwhelming anxiety or sadness that interferes with daily life, consider speaking with a counselor. They're trained to help people navigate changes.
3. **Support Groups:** For certain transitions—like relocating to a new country or dealing with health changes—online or local support groups can connect you with others who've faced similar challenges.

Balancing Optimism and Realism

It's healthy to hope for a positive outcome, but also wise to prepare for bumps along the way. This balanced outlook keeps you from being discouraged by small setbacks. If you start a new job expecting zero difficulties, you might be shocked by normal challenges. On the other hand, if you assume everything will fail, you'll stress yourself unnecessarily.

Recognizing your emotional reactions is part of respecting the fact that change affects you deeply. By naming your emotions, allowing a balance of worry and excitement, and seeking the support you need, you become better equipped to face the transition with courage. In the following sections, we'll explore strategies to practically adapt to change—both in everyday life and larger-scale shifts.

Section 3: Practical Strategies for Navigating Change

1. Gather Information

When you face a major change—like moving schools, switching careers, or relocating—gathering relevant information can reduce uncertainty. If you're changing schools, learn about the new curriculum, clubs, and environment. For a job change, read about the company culture or the new role's responsibilities. Knowledge often replaces fear with clarity.

2. Plan and Organize

1. **Make a Timeline:** Outline important dates or deadlines linked to the change. For example, if you're moving house, list packing days, final utility payments, and moving dates.
2. **Set Mini-Goals:** Instead of focusing on one huge transition, break it down. For instance, if you're starting at a new workplace, aim to learn the main tasks in the first week, get to know at least three coworkers by the second week, and find a comfortable lunch spot by the end of the month.
3. **Create Checklists:** Checklists can keep you on track during chaotic transitions. Mark off each step as you complete it. This also gives a small sense of accomplishment, reducing stress.

3. Maintain a Sense of Routine

Even if your life is in flux, having a few stable routines helps anchor you. You might keep the same morning exercise schedule or continue a Saturday hobby. These consistent habits act as steady pillars amidst change, reminding you that not everything is different.

4. Stay Flexible

Plans are great, but expect the unexpected. Maybe shipping of your belongings gets delayed or your new school's schedule changes last minute. Adapting means you can shift your approach without panicking. Take a breath, think of alternative options, and accept that some parts of change are beyond your control.

5. Build a Support System

1. **Network in the New Environment:** If you're at a new school or job, look for clubs, events, or social groups. Making friends or finding mentors can speed up the settling-in process.
2. **Keep Old Connections Alive:** Communicate with friends or family from your previous environment, especially if they provided emotional support. You don't have to lose old bonds just because you've moved on.

3. **Ask for Help:** Don't be afraid to say, "I'm new here. Could you show me how to fill out these forms?" or "I don't know how to get around yet—could you recommend a bus route?" People are often willing to assist newcomers.

6. Self-Reflection and Growth Mindset

- **Journal Your Progress:** Write down daily or weekly reflections. What went well? What was challenging? This helps you see improvements and adapt faster.
- **Celebrate Milestones:** If you accomplish a small victory—like making a new friend or successfully navigating a tough project—recognize it. Positive reinforcement encourages you to keep trying.

By blending information-gathering, careful planning, flexible thinking, and social support, you can turn major changes into more manageable transitions. Each step you take—whether it's creating a thorough checklist, joining a new club, or calmly adjusting a plan—builds your confidence in handling life's unexpected twists. Next, we'll consider how to use the lessons from past changes to become even more adaptable in the future.

Section 4: Turning Challenges into Opportunities

Change can feel disruptive, but it often opens doors to **new possibilities**. By shifting your perspective and asking, "What can I gain from this?" you transform challenges into chances for learning and personal growth.

Embracing a Growth Mindset

1. **Focus on Learning:** If you're relocating to another city, you might discover a new local culture or learn new navigation skills. If you're changing your job role, you gain fresh expertise. Recognizing these benefits keeps your motivation high.

2. **Appreciate Setbacks:** When you stumble, view it as feedback. For example, if you botch a project at your new job, note what went wrong and plan how to do better next time. This shift from blaming yourself to learning is key to long-term success.

Skill Development

1. **Adaptability Skills:** Handling changes improves your resilience—like strengthening a muscle. Future transitions become less daunting because you've succeeded before.
2. **Communication:** In new situations, you learn how to introduce yourself, make connections, and articulate needs effectively. This fosters better social and negotiation skills.
3. **Problem-Solving:** Changes often come with unforeseen obstacles. Navigating them hones critical thinking, creativity, and resourcefulness.

Social and Professional Advantages

1. **Expanded Network:** Moving to a different school or job exposes you to people with varied backgrounds. Some may become close friends, mentors, or even future business partners.
2. **Higher Adaptability in the Workplace:** Companies value employees who can adapt to new technologies, reorganizations, or shifting markets. Demonstrating a track record of successful transitions can boost your career.

Emotional Growth

1. **Confidence Boost:** Each challenge you overcome—like successfully settling into a new place—reinforces your belief in your own abilities.
2. **Enhanced Empathy:** Going through hard transitions can make you more understanding toward others facing their own changes. You might become a source of comfort or guidance for friends in similar situations.

3. **Greater Self-Awareness:** Major life shifts force you to examine your preferences, habits, and values. You learn what truly matters to you and what you can let go of.

Finding Hidden Opportunities

- **Redefining Goals:** Maybe your move reveals a passion for local volunteering or a subject area you never considered. Use the chance to explore and refine your life's direction.
- **Experimenting Safely:** In a new environment, you can try new hobbies, adopt different routines, or reinvent aspects of your personal style without feeling bound by old expectations.
- **Building Resilience for Future Changes:** After one successful adaptation, you'll approach future changes with more optimism, recalling how you managed last time.

Understanding that change can lead to growth doesn't erase every worry, but it provides a guiding light. Whenever you feel overwhelmed, remind yourself of the skills, contacts, and personal strength you could gain from this transition. This mindset makes it easier to persevere through the uncomfortable phases and come out stronger on the other side.

Section 5: Maintaining Stability During Turbulent Times

It's one thing to adapt to a planned change—a new job you deliberately applied for, a college you chose to attend. But life can also throw unplanned challenges: layoffs, health crises, or sudden family issues. During these **turbulent times**, finding ways to maintain stability is critical to preserving mental health and preventing chaos from overtaking your daily life.

Anchor Points

1. **Keep Some Routines:** If your family is dealing with a serious illness, you might not control the hospital visits or doctor's appointments.

But you can still keep your morning walk or evening journaling routine. Such small constants ground you when larger events are unpredictable.
2. **Return to Hobbies or Soothing Activities:** Even short moments of engagement in painting, reading, or cooking can provide relief from ongoing stress. They act as mini-escapes that reset your emotions.

Financial Security (When Possible)

If the change involves financial strain (like job loss):

- **Review Budget:** Trim unnecessary expenses temporarily. Focus on essentials—housing, food, utilities.
- **Seek Temporary Help:** Government assistance, local charities, or family loans can stabilize you while you search for new opportunities.
- **Update Your Skills:** Free online tutorials or workshops might boost your employability if you need a new income source.

Emotional and Social Support

1. **Lean on Trusted Individuals:** Whether it's a close friend, a sibling, or a mentor, share your worries and progress. You're less likely to feel alone with support by your side.
2. **Professional Counseling:** If the situation is severe—like grieving a loss or experiencing intense anxiety—therapy can offer coping strategies and an unbiased perspective.
3. **Community Resources:** Places of worship, local community centers, or online groups may have support programs or just a friendly circle where you can talk about struggles.

Healthy Coping Instead of Harmful Escape

- **Avoid Substance Abuse:** Stress might tempt you to numb your feelings with alcohol or drugs, but that only postpones problems and can create new ones.
- **Channel Energy Productively:** If you feel restless, direct that energy into cleaning, reorganizing, or home repairs you've postponed. A sense of productivity boosts morale.

Flexibility in Goals

Turbulent times often mean you must pause certain ambitions temporarily. That's okay. Maybe you can't focus on taking extra classes right now because you need to care for a sick relative. Accept that a slower path to your goal is still progress. Reevaluate your timelines and adjust. This flexibility prevents you from feeling like a failure when life's unexpected demands intervene.

Positive Self-Talk

Telling yourself "I'm doing the best I can under these conditions" can counterbalance negative thoughts like "I should be handling this better." Self-compassion is vital. Turbulent times test your limits, but they can also illuminate strengths you didn't know you had. Praising yourself for each small victory (like handling a tough phone call or staying calm in a tense moment) encourages resilience.

By anchoring yourself with stable routines, supportive relationships, financial caution, and healthy coping methods, you create a life raft in the midst of turbulent waters. While you can't always control the storms, you can control how you respond, maintaining a sense of inner steadiness until calmer days arrive.

Section 6: Embracing Change as a Lifelong Skill

Change isn't a one-time event; it's a constant companion throughout life. After you adapt to one shift, another might be waiting just around the corner. **Embracing change as a lifelong skill** transforms what could be an exhausting cycle into a dynamic journey filled with discovery and personal growth.

Lifelong Learning

1. **Stay Curious:** Keep exploring new ideas, technologies, or trends even if you don't need them right now. A flexible, inquisitive mind adapts more easily.

2. **Professional Development:** In a fast-changing job market, continuous skill-building keeps you competitive. Attending workshops, watching tutorials, or pursuing certifications can future-proof your career.
3. **Personal Growth:** Similarly, learning a musical instrument, a second language, or mastering cooking techniques can enrich your life and boost confidence.

Regular Self-Reflection

- **Assess Past Transitions:** Think about previous changes you've managed. What worked well? What challenges did you struggle with? This reflection helps refine your approach for the next shift.
- **Identify Patterns:** Maybe you notice you always resist at first, then gradually accept new situations. Recognizing your typical reaction pattern can help you manage it more smoothly next time.

Keeping an Open Mind

- **Adapt Strategies:** A technique that worked for one type of change might not work for another. For instance, strict planning helps for a planned job shift, but a surprise medical diagnosis might demand more emotional support and less rigid scheduling.
- **Seek Diverse Perspectives:** Chat with friends or mentors who have gone through similar changes. They might offer insights you haven't considered.
- **Avoid Rigid Thinking:** Telling yourself, "I can't handle this" or "I never do well with changes" can become a self-fulfilling prophecy. Stay open to possibilities.

Building a Resilient Identity

- **Define Core Values:** Some aspects of yourself remain steady even during big life changes—such as honesty, kindness, creativity, or determination. Knowing these values keeps you anchored.
- **Experiment Safely:** Trying different styles of communication, leadership, or hobbies can reveal new facets of your identity you might enjoy.

- **Accept Ebb and Flow:** There will be periods of rapid change and times of relative calm. Recognize that life has seasons. Lean into growth when changes arise, and appreciate the stability when it's present.

Teaching Others to Adapt

As you gain experience, you can help children, friends, or coworkers learn adaptability. Sharing your stories—what helped you overcome fear or solve problems—fosters a culture that views change as normal. Encouraging younger people to experiment with new hobbies or step out of their comfort zones builds their confidence early.

Cultivating Optimism

Over time, repeated success in adapting to changes—small or large—creates an optimistic outlook. You'll approach future challenges with less dread and more curiosity. This doesn't mean ignoring risks or potential downsides. Rather, it means acknowledging them but also seeing that you have the tools to navigate the transition.

Embracing change as a continuing part of life requires humility, persistence, and willingness to keep learning. It shifts your mindset from "I hate disruptions" to "I can grow from this," allowing you to remain resilient and hopeful no matter what new chapter unfolds next.

Chapter 19: Continuing Personal Growth Over a Lifetime

Introduction

Many people see personal growth as a goal that they can finish—like graduating from school or completing a project. However, true self-improvement is not a single event or milestone. It is a **lifelong process** that continues as we move through different stages of life. Childhood, teenage years, adulthood, and later life all offer new opportunities to learn and develop. Even when we feel we have gained a high level of skill or wisdom, there is always more to explore and master.

In previous chapters, we discussed many ways to become better—managing time, facing stress, nurturing relationships, adapting to change, and so on. Here, in **Chapter 19**, we will look more deeply at how personal growth can continue throughout your life. We will examine why it is not enough just to learn a skill once and then stop. We will see how curiosity and reflection can keep pushing you forward. We will also talk about how to adapt your goals as you grow older, how to handle the feeling of being stuck or hitting plateaus, and why sharing your journey with mentors, friends, or communities can keep you motivated.

By the end of this chapter, you will understand that self-improvement does not end at a certain age. Instead, it becomes a natural part of living if you maintain an open mind and a willingness to keep learning. You will see that the excitement of life comes in part from discovering new talents, tackling fresh challenges, and refining your character year after year. Let's dive into the idea of **continuing personal growth over a lifetime** and see how you can keep moving forward, no matter which stage of life you find yourself in.

Section 1: Personal Growth Is Not a Destination

Growth as a Lifelong Journey

Many people think about improvement in terms of finishing a race—like if they can just lose weight, get a promotion, or finish a big project, they will be "done." However, real personal growth is more like a winding path with no end point. You do not "graduate" from being a better person. Each time you reach a goal, you find there are new skills to learn or different areas to explore.

Embracing Continuous Learning

If you imagine someone who masters one subject—say, mathematics—they do not stop learning just because they have a degree. They might discover new branches of math, want to teach others, or apply their knowledge to physics, engineering, or economics. The same is true for any field of knowledge. Once you see that there is always more to master, you realize that growth never really stops.

Even in your personal life—like building empathy, leadership, or healthy habits—there is no finish line. You might get very good at communicating, only to realize you still struggle when stressed or dealing with unfamiliar cultures. This realization is not discouraging if you see learning as an adventure. Rather than being upset there is more to do, you can feel excited that life always offers new lessons.

The Risk of Complacency

Complacency is a state of being too satisfied with your current achievements, which can halt your progress. Sometimes, after reaching a big goal, people stop pushing themselves. They might think, "I have done enough." While it is healthy to celebrate milestones, staying complacent can mean missing out on fresh experiences and improvements.

Also, life changes rapidly. The world you live in today will not be the same tomorrow. Technology, society, and even your own body and mind evolve over time. If you stay where you are, you risk falling behind or becoming stuck while everything else moves forward. Continuous growth ensures you can keep pace, remain adaptable, and find meaning in each new chapter of life.

Growth in Different Life Stages

A teenager might focus on learning to study effectively, make friends, or handle peer pressure. A young adult could be developing career skills, handling finances, or building deeper relationships. Middle-aged individuals might emphasize career advancement, family care, or personal hobbies they put off earlier. Seniors can focus on sharing wisdom, mentoring the younger generation, and finding fulfillment in retirement activities. Each stage has its unique growth opportunities.

Section 2: The Role of Curiosity and Lifelong Learning

Curiosity as Fuel

One key to continuous personal growth is **curiosity**. Curious people ask questions, try new activities, and seek knowledge beyond what they currently know. This sense of wonder can lead you to discover hidden talents, explore fresh hobbies, or solve problems in inventive ways. Without curiosity, life can become dull and repetitive. With it, even everyday experiences can reveal something new.

When curiosity drives you, learning stops being a chore and becomes a natural habit. You find yourself reading about topics outside your main field, attending workshops just because they sound interesting, or experimenting with creative arts that spark your imagination. This constant flow of new ideas can open doors you never knew existed.

Lifelong Learning Approaches

1. **Reading Broadly:** Do not just read in your area of expertise. Dip into different genres—history, science, biography, philosophy, or even children's literature. Each type of book can offer insights or spark creativity.
2. **Online Courses and Tutorials:** The internet provides countless platforms—many free—that teach skills from coding to guitar playing. Even as an adult, taking an online course can refresh your knowledge or introduce you to a brand-new field.
3. **Hobbies and Extracurriculars:** Learning to paint, garden, cook international dishes, or fix computers may seem like random pursuits, but they can sharpen your mind and add layers to your personality. They also reduce stress and enrich your life.
4. **Asking Questions:** When you meet someone with an interesting job or a unique background, ask questions about their experiences. You may pick up tips or find a mentor. Curiosity can also strengthen social bonds, as people usually enjoy talking about what they know well.

Overcoming Learning Blocks

Adults often believe they are "too old" to learn new skills or that their brain cannot handle complex topics. Research shows that while the brain does change with age, it remains capable of acquiring new knowledge. Yes, it might take more time or practice, but the benefits—staying mentally sharp, discovering fresh passions—are huge. Children face their own blocks too, such as fear of failure or peer judgment. In both cases, you can replace self-doubt with a growth mindset: you are not "bad" at something; you are just not experienced yet.

Lifelong Learning Communities

Sharing the learning journey with others can keep you motivated. Clubs, discussion groups, and community classes allow you to learn together, exchange ideas, and encourage each other through difficulties. Even online forums can provide support. Feeling part of a learning community helps you stay excited and accountable.

Section 3: Reflection and Self-Assessment

Why Reflection Matters

Personal growth is easier to sustain if you regularly **reflect** on what you have learned and how you have changed. Reflection means looking back on your experiences, evaluating your successes and failures, and deciding what to do next. Without it, you might keep repeating the same mistakes or miss opportunities to celebrate progress. Reflection also helps you spot areas where you feel unfulfilled, pushing you to set new goals or adjust your direction.

Methods of Reflection

1. **Journaling:** Writing in a journal is a classic way to process your thoughts. Jot down achievements, struggles, and emotional responses. Over time, you can read past entries to see how you have evolved.
2. **Mind Mapping:** If you prefer visual methods, create a map of your recent experiences, linking them to lessons learned. This can highlight patterns you did not notice before.
3. **Conversation Partners:** Sometimes, reflecting with a friend or mentor who knows you well can be insightful. Talking out loud helps clarify what is going on in your mind. A trusted person might offer a different angle on your experiences.
4. **Yearly Reviews or "Life Audits":** Once a year, you can do a bigger review: list your top wins, regrets, and lessons from the past 12 months. Then plan how you want the next year to go. This is especially helpful when you are thinking about bigger life transitions.

Being Honest with Yourself

Reflection works only if you are **truthful** about your behaviors, emotions, and challenges. Denying problems or blaming others might feel more comfortable, but it stops you from seeing how you can grow. Admitting mistakes or areas of weakness might sting at first, yet it is the best way to break bad habits and keep improving.

Avoiding Perfectionism

Sometimes, reflection can lead to harsh self-criticism if you fixate on what you did "wrong." Balance this by noting what you did right, too. Personal growth includes recognizing small victories and acknowledging that no one is perfect. The goal is not to tear yourself down but to understand yourself more deeply and guide future actions.

Creating an Action Plan

After reflecting, turn insights into **action**. If you realize you keep procrastinating on certain tasks, decide on concrete steps to change that—like setting earlier deadlines or using a reward system. If you see you have neglected a friendship, schedule a meetup or call. Reflection without action might enlighten you, but it will not bring much change.

Section 4: Overcoming Plateaus and Boredom

Understanding Plateaus

Even with a growth mindset, you may hit **plateaus**—periods where you feel stuck and see little progress. Maybe you no longer feel challenged at work, or your guitar practice does not seem to improve your skills. Plateaus can lead to boredom, frustration, or the temptation to quit. Recognizing these stages is crucial for breaking through them.

Reasons for Plateaus

1. **Lack of Challenge:** If tasks become too easy, your mind does not stay engaged. You might stop learning new techniques or pushing your limits.
2. **Repeated Routines:** Doing the same workout or study method for too long can slow progress because your body or brain adapts and gets less benefit from the same activity.

3. **Insufficient Feedback or Mentorship:** Sometimes, not having fresh input from a teacher, coach, or peer group leaves you uncertain about how to improve.
4. **Burnout or Overwork:** If you are exhausted, your ability to learn or perform at a high level might stall.

Strategies to Break Through

1. **Add Variety:** Change your approach. If you are an artist, explore a new style or medium. If you are studying math, try different problem sets or tutoring someone else to view concepts differently.
2. **Set a Bigger Challenge:** If your job no longer challenges you, ask for more responsibility, start a side project, or apply for a position that stretches your abilities. When you aim higher, you have new hurdles to overcome, which can reignite growth.
3. **Seek Guidance:** Find a mentor or instructor who can offer a new perspective. They might pinpoint small errors or gaps you never noticed.
4. **Measure Progress in New Ways:** If your usual metrics do not show improvement, try different measurements. For instance, if your weight training plateaued, track muscle endurance or daily energy levels instead of just weight-lifting gains.

Reigniting Motivation

- **Remember Your Purpose:** Why did you start this journey? Reflecting on your deeper reasons can restore your enthusiasm.
- **Reward Yourself:** Set milestones and give yourself small treats or breaks when you meet them. Rewards can keep you pushing forward.
- **Rediscover Fun:** If self-improvement feels stale, reintroduce playful elements. Gamify your goals, compete with a friend, or learn in a group that shares your passion.

Knowing When to Pivot

Sometimes, a plateau might signal that it is time to shift direction. For example, if you realize you no longer enjoy a certain hobby or career path, it might not be a simple plateau but a sign you need new challenges in a different field. Reflect on whether you are truly stuck or if your interests have changed.

Section 5: Mentors, Role Models, and Community

Why Outside Support Matters

Although personal growth is often seen as an individual pursuit, **mentors**, **role models**, and **community** can significantly shape your path. They offer guidance, motivation, and diverse viewpoints that you might not discover on your own. Having supportive people around you can also provide accountability, ensuring you do not give up easily.

Finding Mentors

1. **Teachers and Experts:** People who have achieved what you aim for—like a seasoned musician or a skilled engineer—can give direct advice and help you avoid common pitfalls.
2. **Online Communities:** In the digital age, mentors can be found online. Forums, social media groups, or educational platforms often host knowledgeable individuals willing to share tips.
3. **Workplace Mentorship Programs:** Many companies have structured programs pairing newer employees with experienced staff. This can speed your professional development.

Role Models vs. Mentors

A **role model** is someone you admire, whose life or achievements inspire you. You might not know them personally—like a famous athlete or an author. By observing their traits, you can adopt certain habits or mindsets. Meanwhile, a **mentor** is someone you can actually interact with, ask questions, and receive personalized feedback from. Role models provide inspiration, while mentors give hands-on guidance.

Building a Growth Community

- **Peer Groups:** Sometimes, friends or classmates on the same journey can become your "growth community." You learn together, swap resources, and encourage one another.
- **Family and Close Friends:** Even if they do not share the same goals, loving family members can offer moral support, celebrate your wins, and comfort you when you struggle.
- **Professional Associations or Clubs:** Joining local clubs (like a writers' circle or a coding group) or professional bodies can broaden your network and deepen your expertise.

Staying Open to Feedback

A community or mentor's advice only helps if you **listen** with an open mind. Some feedback may be tough to swallow—like pointing out weaknesses you have overlooked—but that is often what propels major growth. Try to evaluate the suggestions fairly and see how they fit your context.

Giving Back

Personal growth is not just about receiving. Eventually, you may find yourself in a position to **mentor** or **advise** others. Sharing what you have learned cements your own knowledge and feels rewarding. It also continues the cycle of growth, as your mentee might bring fresh perspectives that inspire you in return.

Section 6: Adapting Goals Over Time

Why Goals Evolve

At different life stages, your **priorities and circumstances change**. Perhaps you focused on academic success as a teenager. Then in your 20s, career goals took center stage. Later, family life or personal health may become your biggest concern. Clinging to old goals that no longer fit your current reality can lead to frustration or a sense of emptiness. Growth means adapting your ambitions to match who you are now and what you truly need.

Reviewing and Updating Goals

1. **Schedule Regular Goal Check-Ins:** Every few months, or at least yearly, review your goals. Ask yourself if they are still relevant, achievable, and aligned with your values.
2. **Remove or Transform Obsolete Goals:** Maybe you wanted to run a marathon, but after a knee injury, you must shift to swimming. Adjust the goal to match new conditions.
3. **Add Fresh Objectives:** If you discover a budding interest in cooking, create a new goal: "Try at least one new recipe each week" or "Enroll in a cooking class." This keeps life exciting.

Balancing Short-Term and Long-Term

- **Short-Term Goals:** These might last a few weeks or months, like improving your daily routine or finishing a specific project. They provide immediate satisfaction and keep you motivated.
- **Long-Term Goals:** Spanning years or even decades, such goals give you direction—saving money for a house, building a career in a certain field, or mastering a complex skill.
- **Mixing Both:** Successful personal growth often combines these two types. Short-term achievements serve as stepping stones toward bigger, long-term visions.

Staying Flexible

When you see obstacles or changes in your environment—a global economic shift, family responsibilities, health issues—**flexibility** prevents you from feeling you have "failed." Instead of giving up, you adapt. For instance, if a business plan fails due to market shifts, you do not discard your dream of entrepreneurship. You change the product line, target market, or approach, learning from the setback.

The Value of Letting Go

Sometimes, letting go of a long-cherished goal is hard but necessary. Maybe your dream was to become a professional athlete, but injuries or personal choices have made that impractical. Grieving that lost dream is normal, but forcing yourself to keep chasing it can block you from new, more suitable goals. Embracing the release of old ambitions can free your energy to flourish elsewhere.

Checking Alignment with Values

As you set or modify goals, ensure they match your **core values**—things like family, creativity, independence, or service to others. If a goal conflicts with what you deeply care about, you might struggle to remain motivated. Aligning goals with values not only keeps you driven but also brings a sense of fulfillment beyond external success.

Chapter 20: Conclusion: A New Path Forward

Introduction

We have come a long way in this book, exploring many areas of personal growth—setting clear goals, building discipline, communicating effectively, nurturing relationships, facing stress, balancing work and personal life, adapting to change, and more. Each chapter provided strategies and mindsets to help you become the best version of yourself. Now, in **Chapter 20**, we bring everything together to form **a new path forward**.

In this conclusion, we will review the core principles that weave through all these topics. You will see how self-awareness, kindness, responsibility, and a growth mindset unite to support every effort toward bettering yourself. We will also look at how to handle setbacks and unforeseen obstacles, understanding that personal growth is not always linear. Sometimes you move two steps forward and one step back—but that does not mean you fail. It is simply how real growth often happens.

By the end of this chapter, you will have a clear picture of how these lessons combine into a lifelong plan for improvement, resilience, and joy. You will be reminded that the journey is ongoing, that small daily acts make a significant impact, and that sharing your progress with others can multiply its effects. Let us now tie all these threads together, affirming that the quest to be better is not just about reaching goals but about embracing a more meaningful, compassionate, and adaptable way of living.

Section 1: Recap of Key Insights

Setting Goals and Building Discipline

Early in the book, we discussed how **setting clear, meaningful goals** and backing them with discipline can help you transform your dreams into tangible outcomes. Whether the aim is to improve grades, develop a skill, or get fit, making your goals **specific**, **measurable**, and **time-bound** keeps you on track. Discipline then helps you persist when motivation dips.

Facing Fears and Developing Healthy Habits

Fear and doubt often hold people back. However, we learned that recognizing your fears, breaking them into manageable steps, and taking small actions can weaken their power. This goes hand in hand with creating **healthy daily habits**—like proper nutrition, regular exercise, and responsible self-care—that maintain energy, reduce stress, and support a calmer mindset.

Communication, Relationships, and Kindness

Another central theme was how effective **communication**—being clear, respectful, and a good listener—builds stronger relationships. Sharing your thoughts openly while also valuing others' perspectives nurtures trust. Practicing **gratitude** and **kindness** lifts not just your own spirits, but also those of the people around you. We saw that small acts of thoughtfulness can create a positive ripple in your community.

Stress Management and Work-Life Balance

Stress is unavoidable, but we explored ways to handle it—like time management, relaxation techniques, and setting boundaries. Finding a **work-life balance** ensures you do not burn out, keeps relationships healthy, and allows time for personal joys. Regularly checking in with yourself and ensuring you do not overcommit fosters long-term well-being.

Adapting to Change and Lifelong Growth

We also focused on the fact that life is always changing. Learning to adapt—whether it is relocating to a new place, starting a new career, or facing unexpected events—keeps you flexible. Seeing each change as a chance to learn and improve becomes a cornerstone of personal resilience. With an outlook of **lifelong growth**, you remain open to learning at every age, reflecting on your progress, and adjusting goals as your circumstances or interests shift.

The Core Values Underlying All Topics

Throughout, certain values emerged repeatedly:

- **Responsibility:** Owning your decisions and their results.
- **Openness:** Welcoming new ideas and experiences.
- **Empathy and Respect:** In how you listen, speak, and act.
- **Honesty:** With yourself (through reflection) and with others (through communication).
- **Consistency:** Maintaining good habits and discipline over time.
- **Adaptability:** Letting go of rigid expectations when life changes.

Section 2: Handling Setbacks and Obstacles

Recognizing Setbacks Are Normal

No matter how well you plan, **setbacks** will happen. You might fail an important test, lose a job opportunity, or have conflict in a close relationship. These moments can be discouraging. However, a key lesson from the book is that **failure** does not define you; your reaction to it does. Instead of seeing a setback as the end, view it as an opportunity to learn and refine your methods.

Emotional Management

When obstacles arise, strong emotions like frustration, sadness, or anger are common. Drawing on the stress management techniques covered—deep breathing, grounding methods, or short breaks—can help you calm down and regain focus. If the setback is severe, talking to a friend, mentor, or therapist might be necessary to process the disappointment in a healthy way.

Reassessing Goals

Sometimes, a setback reveals that your original goal or approach needs adjustment. If you aimed to complete a project in three months but realize it is going to take double that time, you can revise the timeline rather than quitting altogether. Being flexible with your goals ensures that you do not throw away your dream just because the initial path was blocked.

Learning from Mistakes

Ask yourself questions like:

- **What exactly went wrong?**
- **Was there something I could have done differently?**
- **Did I overlook any resources or advice that might have helped?**

Answering these honestly helps you avoid repeating the same mistake. It also deepens your understanding of your strengths and weaknesses. For instance, failing a job interview might highlight that you need to practice speaking under pressure or improve your technical knowledge.

Using Criticism Constructively

If a teacher, boss, or friend points out shortcomings, it might sting. But often, this feedback holds clues on how to improve. Even if their tone is harsh, look for the useful part of their critique. Then, decide whether to adopt it fully or adapt it to your situation. This approach keeps you from dismissing helpful advice due to pride or fear.

Rebounding Stronger

A setback can sometimes be the catalyst for bigger growth. It can force you to adopt new methods, seek better mentorship, or step out of your comfort zone in ways you would not have otherwise. This idea parallels the concept of "post-traumatic growth," where a major challenge results in a deeper sense of purpose or understanding of yourself. By staying open-minded, you transform defeats into stepping stones.

Section 3: Small Daily Acts, Big Results

The Power of Incremental Progress

A major theme throughout this book is that **small actions add up**. You do not need to conquer huge tasks every single day to see growth. Instead, steady daily habits—like reading 10 pages of a helpful book, practicing a new language for 15 minutes, or tidying a bit of your living space—accumulate into big changes over time. This approach reduces the pressure to make drastic shifts all at once.

Consistency Over Intensity

Some individuals try intense bursts of effort—studying non-stop for 10 hours, exercising to exhaustion, or drastically dieting for a week—then burn out and revert to old patterns. A more sustainable approach is to do moderately challenging tasks regularly. For instance, exercising 20–30 minutes a day consistently will often produce better results than pushing too hard once in a while.

Examples of Small Acts

1. **Learning:** Solve a couple of math problems daily or watch a short educational video.
2. **Fitness:** Take a brisk walk or do a quick home workout routine each morning.
3. **Relationship Care:** Send a supportive text to a friend, or do a small favor for a family member.
4. **Mindfulness:** Spend 5 minutes practicing deep breathing or meditation each evening before bed.
5. **Organization:** Clean one shelf, answer a few emails, or pay a bill. Breaking tasks into small chunks makes them less daunting.

Tracking and Accountability

- **Habit Trackers:** Using an app or a simple chart to mark when you complete a daily habit can motivate you to maintain streaks.

- **Buddy System:** If you share your goals with a friend, you can check in on each other's progress. This friendly accountability doubles the chance you will stay consistent.

Celebrating Small Victories

When you see that you have practiced the guitar for 10 minutes every day for a month, it is worth **celebrating**. These small victories encourage you to keep going. You might treat yourself to something you enjoy, or simply acknowledge, "I am proud of my consistency." This sense of reward cements the habit.

Long-Term Impact

Over weeks or months, these minor efforts compound into notable achievements. You might find you have read several books, increased your strength, saved money, or improved relationships. This method also teaches you patience and discipline—critical components for long-term growth.

Section 4: Sharing Growth with Others

The Social Dimension of Self-Improvement

Though personal growth is inherently about you, it does not happen in isolation. Your family, friends, coworkers, and community can all benefit from your journey. They can also influence, inspire, or challenge you along the way. Sharing what you have learned fosters connection and helps you internalize lessons more deeply.

Inspiring and Guiding

1. **Role Modeling:** If your younger sibling sees you studying diligently, they might pick up better study habits. If your coworker notices you manage stress calmly, they might adopt some of your strategies.

2. **Workshops or Talks:** If you develop expertise in a hobby—like painting or coding—you can volunteer to teach a short class or hold a mini-workshop. Teaching is a powerful way to solidify your own understanding.
3. **Online Platforms:** Social media, blogs, or forums can be spaces where you share motivational tips or reflect on your personal growth challenges. Doing so might connect you with like-minded individuals.

Accountability Partnerships

We discussed earlier how you can join or form **growth communities**. Within these, you might create partnerships for accountability—regular check-ins where each person discusses progress, obstacles, and next steps. Knowing someone expects an update can boost your motivation to follow through. It also gives you a chance to provide encouragement and feedback to them.

The Risks of Comparisons

While sharing can uplift, it can also tempt comparisons. You might see someone who has progressed faster or in a different way than you, leading to jealousy or self-doubt. To combat this, remember that everyone's journey is unique, with different starting points and challenges. Use others' successes as inspiration rather than a reason to feel behind.

Building a Support Network

- **Collaborative Problem-Solving:** If you face a complex goal, a group's combined experiences can generate ideas you would not have thought of alone.
- **Emotional Encouragement:** On days when you feel stuck, a supportive friend or mentor can remind you how far you have come and that setbacks are normal.
- **Resource Sharing:** People in your network might recommend books, courses, or contacts that help you advance faster.

Spreading Positive Ripples

When you practice kindness, gratitude, and responsibility, those around you may follow suit. One person's improved communication can reduce conflicts in a family or workplace. One student's new approach to studying might spark classmates to adopt better habits. This ripple effect is how individual personal growth contributes to a healthier, happier community or society at large.

Section 5: Creating a Sustainable Roadmap for Life

Combining All the Elements

By now, you have explored many themes: clarity of goals, discipline, healthy habits, communication, gratitude, stress management, resilience, balance, adaptability, and lifelong learning. The question is, **how do you fit them all together** in a sustainable way?

Here is a simplified blueprint:

1. **Identify Your Core Values:** These are qualities or principles—like honesty, compassion, creativity—that matter most to you. Align your goals and habits with these values to ensure your efforts feel meaningful.
2. **Set and Review Goals:** Keep a mix of short-term (daily/weekly) and long-term (months/years) goals. Revisit them periodically to confirm they still reflect your life stage and interests.
3. **Integrate Healthy Habits:** Physical exercise, nutritious eating, proper sleep, and mindfulness form the foundation of a stable mind and body, enabling consistent growth in all areas.
4. **Practice Ongoing Reflection:** Use journaling or personal check-ins. Reflect on what went well, what did not, and why. Make adjustments as needed.

5. **Cultivate Relationships and Community:** Communicate openly, listen actively, and offer kindness or help to others. A supportive network accelerates learning and provides emotional strength.
6. **Manage Stress and Set Boundaries:** Learn to say "no" or delegate when necessary, respect personal time, and apply relaxation or coping strategies to prevent burnout.
7. **Adapt to Change:** Remain flexible. When life shifts, modify your approach, goals, or routines, using each change as a chance to discover new strengths and lessons.
8. **Stay Curious:** Keep reading, exploring new skills, and asking questions. Lifelong learning prevents stagnation and encourages ongoing self-improvement.

Balancing Ambition with Self-Compassion

Ambition can drive progress, but pushing yourself too hard can lead to stress or fatigue. Practice **self-compassion**—acknowledge that you are human, you will make mistakes, and you cannot always function at your peak. Forgiving yourself for off days or slower periods is part of a sustainable plan. This mindset helps you bounce back from missteps rather than quitting when faced with imperfection.

Periodic "Life Audits"

Once or twice a year, do a broad evaluation:

- Are you living in line with your core values?
- Are your key relationships thriving?
- Do your daily habits support your bigger goals, or do they need adjusting?
- What changes or experiments do you want to try next?

These audits keep you updated on your progress and any shifts in your desires or responsibilities.

Conclusion

Reaching the final chapter of this book, you now possess a comprehensive view of **how to be better** in many aspects of life. From disciplined goal-setting and effective communication to managing stress, adapting to change, and learning continuously, each part of this journey shows that personal growth is multi-layered and ongoing. There is no single finish line; there is always another angle to explore, another skill to refine, another step to take toward becoming a wiser, kinder, and more capable person.

We have seen that self-improvement is not about perfection. It is about **consistency** in small, daily choices—building better habits, staying open to feedback, respecting yourself and others, and being willing to make changes when needed. It is also about **community**: sharing your progress with friends, mentors, and loved ones, and inspiring them to grow as you do. It is about **resilience**, facing setbacks and learning from them rather than giving up. And it is about **gratitude and kindness**, recognizing how your actions affect the world around you and offering support whenever you can.

Now, as you step into **a new path forward**, remember that every challenge holds a lesson, every success a moment to celebrate, and every day an opportunity to practice the principles we have covered. Keep reflecting on where you are, keep adjusting your goals to align with your changing values and circumstances, and keep cultivating curiosity. In this way, you ensure that growth remains a steady companion throughout your life, guiding you toward deeper fulfillment, stronger relationships, and a positive impact on your community and beyond.

Thank you for joining this journey. May the insights and strategies within these pages serve you well as you continue to learn, adapt, and become a better version of yourself—today, tomorrow, and over a lifetime.

www.ingramcontent.com/pod-product-compliance
Lightning Source LLC
LaVergne TN
LVHW012038070526
838202LV00056B/5531